FG
BY
FG

HYSTERICAL BOOOKS

FG
BY
FG

HYSTERICAL BOOOKS
TALLAHASSEE, FL
2019

Copyright © Frank Giampietro 2019
All rights reserved under
International and Pan-American Copyright Conventions.

No portion of this book may be reproduced in any form without the written permission of the publisher, except by a reviewer, who may quote brief passages in connection with a review for a magazine or newspaper.

Cover Image: FG by FG

Author photograph: FG
Design, production: Hysterical Books
Library of Congress Cataloging-in-Publication Data
FG by FG by Frank Giampietro — First Edition
ISBN — 978-0-940821-10-1

Hysterical Books is dedicated to the
publication and appreciation of fine poetry and other literary genres.

HYSTERICAL BOOKS
Email: hystericalbooks@gmail.com
Published in the United States by Hysterical Books
Hysterical Books is an imprint of Apalachee Press
Tallahassee, Florida • First Edition, 2019

DEDICATION
for my beloved family

FG
BY
FG

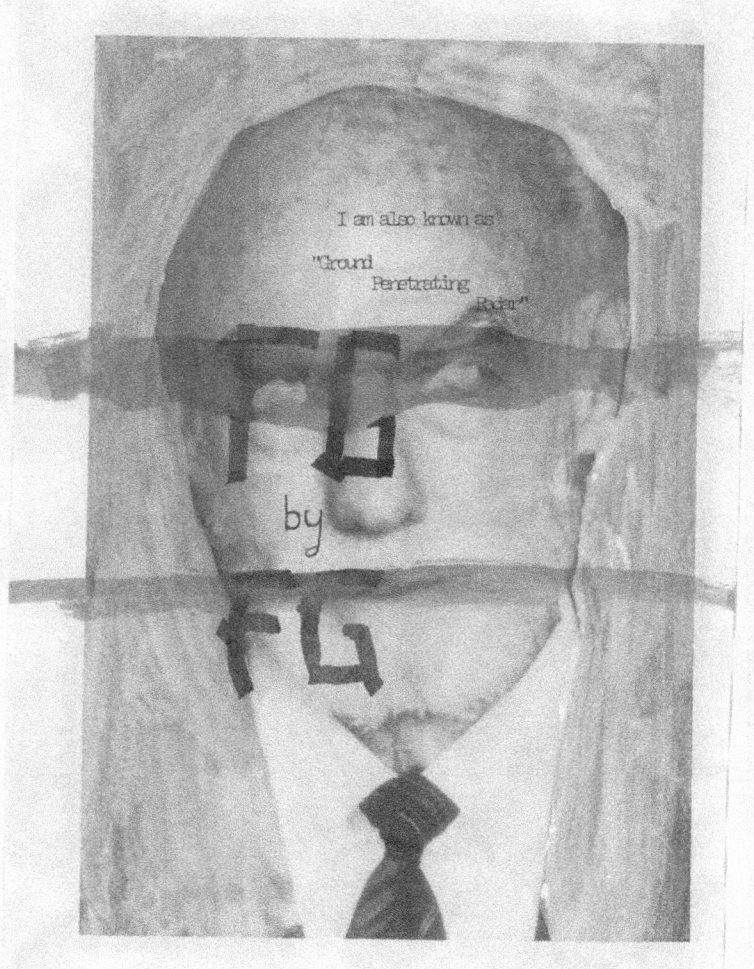

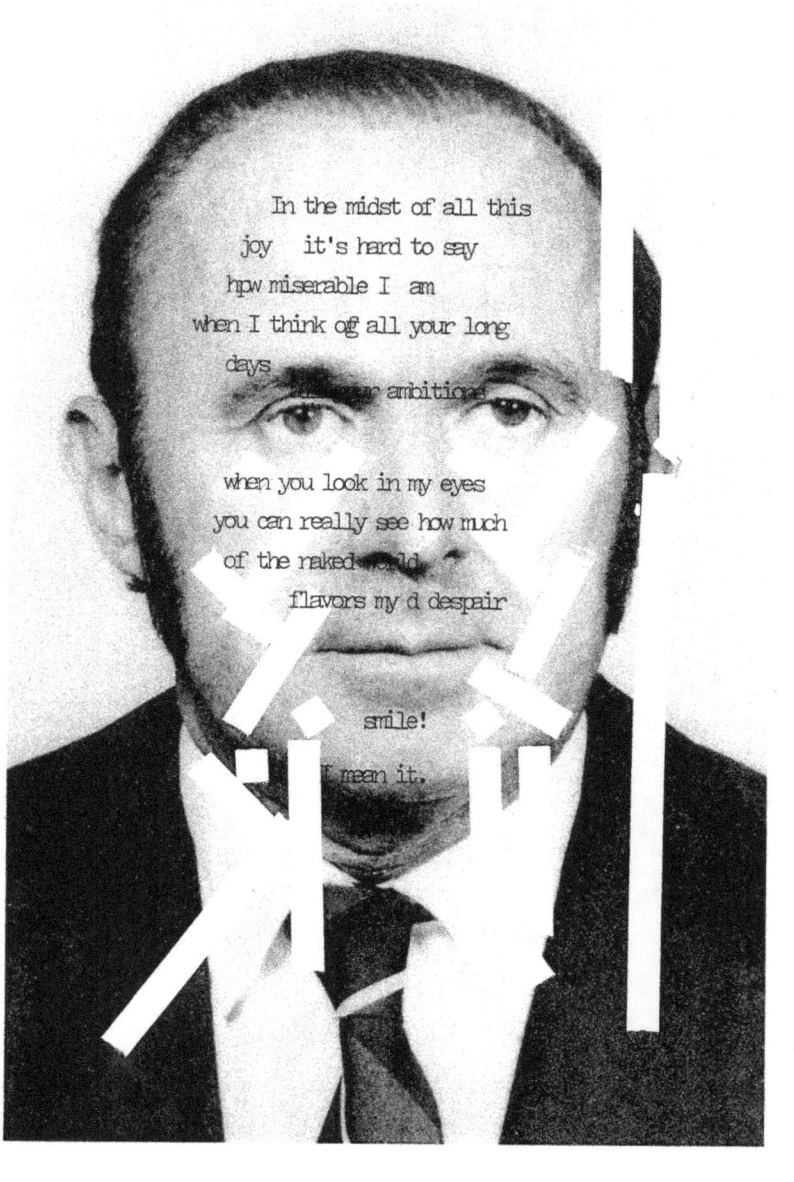

JOKES & NAMES
by fg

Just before I started this I was thinking about taking my pile of other peoples, ms. and dividing them into tiny stacks and forming those stacks into type in all caps on my oriental runner which isn,t my runner but my my sister,s stepdaughters, runner because it belonged to their mom wgo died and that s all you say ab out thw dead wgen you are talking on this here machine . So what if I can just direct all the times I,ve everr tried to talk to a macs backs bookstore clerks, lemony covers. This is free, right? So i made the P on the runner , THE runner andi took a picture of it anddid notmpost it to fa ebook. But it,s on the cloud. "fg's Unposted"

I'm allowed spaced paragraphs , says I. knowing its says you. Which reminds me tha onerule has to bethat I do not scr ap the whole project if I happen to get either , NOT eitherIf I happen to star t gettingall the world is either oneway or its thisother then I will forgive myself and just get right back to sincerity which I'veplenty of, Baby. . .

Gravity wasdumb says the reporter. My brother says stand for something or you might die for an ything. So the questio is can i write a phrase like o the absurdity of life? andit would affect you as it effects cha ge. ?? Tonight i watched a video on Lynda.com and tonight i tried to record a song on Garage Band but it was too hard. Just thinking that deeply in thosetermd it8s wha sepatates the harvard from the jail. But here I am noy mindingthis so much and the reader whor isy ou will see me evrey single time I go flowery andth at is tension. tha is a bAnch of keys gettingstuck at the gae just before Jesus says flowery heaven.   BTW, cool indi directors say theword fuck more often then sincerity demands and AND they are fat smart dumb andloud andyou forgive them.
Our hero does forgive them who d id choose the life and well being od a sta ger than oneamongitsmidst. s ? Boring , bored . But beforeI go knowthat I shall return becauze if I don't I'll be a sweet potato, which is what I'm eaing for dinn r Fbook.

I think I'm in love" said thelonius beckhandson

Still in love
Upper twenties and teens for the rest of another Cleve LAND week.
My mom kindof can't believe I hae a PhD. At fir t I was like yesthat's miy
niche. But bla bla bla BTW her is another rule. When I go bla bla bla that
meansI'm almost goingto givethisshit up like a butt plugg on movi gday .
I still haven'thad the sweet potato but I shall whe it is hascookeatwice baked
if you will that 's what she said and GIRLS isso crzy wrd andwhat better word
to spekl incorrectly superciliousness actually no i jus wnted to try t.hat
word too. The wordis"solypcystical " which islike test icicle which Im
here by coining "tes icicle": A combination of my butt.

Onemorething before I watch interesti gly GIRLS I'm a little bit worri4 d
 that thisidea which is to writ e onepage of t his on every day of my exi.e
andoncemy exile is pve r that isonceI am reuntied with my family and have
avhievedan other andmore stable form of employment , on tha day I shall
takepicturs of this andnot post any ofit to Facebook $$'

Oh or I will finis this whe I am finished writgng on every single pie ce
of ms paper whic I did reject as an editor of such a place tha does excepy
mss at $25 a pop. Thisnot what I am after.
So onemorething whileIm at it and tha is to refer you to a little book caled
lettersto a you gPoet by Signor Rilke. (I will try to not seem so s tupied)
R says the
    one

Typing typeing isa dactly ycursive my butt.

If you got atbleast three iambs ina 10 beat line thenyou got yourself iambic
pentameter.
This I believe.
I believe that a semic·lon has the function .
Dear, Typewriter Fixer, I am typeinf very methodically to test this keyboard
to see howfast I ca type wit out the spacebar notspacing as it houlf and ale
w:.a combination ofletters, etc.

The swift beown fox jumpedovermy butt.
The swift brown fox jumped over the wood.
The swift brown foc jumped onto my jock.

The prec3din g was a demonstartion of theruleof 3s. A rul e whichI continue
to havefifficulw explaing whats interesti g ab out it becajuse for one tning
I can not rememb:r j okes. Jokesna·amesare the teo I can'/wont do.
 AND
    we have a title.'

Sweet potato. I shall now eat and tha shall bring us the memory of it earlier in our bla bla bla

Thesweet otato w_as delicious. The 4th episode of GIRLS is awesome. : One Man's trash. She Le'na is doing a meta holden caulfield and also: she is really good with the imagesandI get now why we have to start with shocking It's like my blue middle fingernail. It says fuck you but on a bif mety mail albeit liberal male hand andi ts like theunshelled almonds on my faux counter top which reminds me that my cost per hour is morethan say a trip to the Home D epot or Gods store or saturday birdhouse making class in Baton Rouge memory of timewith my childrent ht worked oyut well, tha is no kids under the giant aisles andpolished cement tha I oncewantedon the floo ofmy whole home .

I haefire ants andtherefore I hat e the south,. There .
A boring bori ng· boring bori ng b ored boy who had cha ged his mind whyhe ha d sobered up cameino the kitchen tha morning to findlittle morethn some dirty dirty dish si the sink.

should not go up to any old cvsemployees and be friendly whe n and becaus e they do not need your friendshi p and you are foisti g onto them something bla bSo what if I said cvs employees are shit dumb stu pid asses ever I would of courze just bekiddng. ButIfI said it on FB I would get friends. The carriage of the typewriter knovked over a bottle of cvs norishing blue fingernail polish remover. Theit knocke over the dumb beer and then the bowl of unsheloed almonds which I happen to hav eright here no thereit goes. No I do and thats means nice. Note to self do not hide the en of your thought s in a childish in on cents , I makedelicious pudding. If a character says to m other characyer tha: she si too narcisitical to kill herslef and he is supposee to b bedeep then I don't know what's wghat. Indeed I'm not the forest Gump of brilliant artisis/thinkers/poets I'm Brett Easton Ellisof litersry poetry pop hip 44 year old , dude. Sandfa Bullock is the most clearly rtagic example of how not to look as you continue to age that I have ev r noticed befor e. NoteNASA Blind every fucking body hzs seen falling stars recently and all of them have thought it a good omen of t h future an they hav eall been wrong. Probably a fucking chainrea ting sattelite
 FuckingGeorge fucking bla bla bl a thi s concludes my Brett EAstonEllis review of t both the tv show GIRLS and the podcast andpersoality ofBrett Easton Ellis who m Iam like more tha n I am like forest Gump the only difference being I am n ot famously famous for being famous and cool i n thaLA sort of bla bla bla

So I have decided th t I don't even care if what I say tells a good story
or hasriding action or begins with did I ever tell you the story of George
Clooney in New Orleons or Paul Giamoyyi selling slavezi the hood.
So, if I am edi ti ngor not editing then does that mean I have to say that
I realize this isn't befinning very well today and the whole "hoodW" monent
was terriblean regrettable.? The video I watched today call d 29 things to
sta creative mentioned that not be aing yourself up was important. SO, okay.
So if I am 44 can I still say I am growin. and getting better at things
like livi ng alone and knowing how much of my parishable food to buy at the
grocery store. ? Andif it's overall good that I am not eating as much processed
food and I am spending considerably more time cleaning up after myself and mki g
the bedevery day amd kep the sink free of pots , does that m an I am happi r
than I have been in a while andtherefor e am more likey to appreciate wgatevr
successes I have fro m here on ? In an internet tes I took hismorning tha
t tells you wh kid of philospheryou are it said that I am an exostentialist
egoist. I bee you w sh I startedwith the sentenve . whomeve ryou are.
Somebody lucky enough that people would listen to his opinions saif ust
the only reaso n he is successful is because he knows what people think 2 minutes
beforethey do. I think it was think. Maybehe said heknows what people will do
2 minut sbefirethey do. Whatever it is I get it and tnhough I fail at
this same --See, I hte howthat was startingto sound. It started to sound
unlovely then ego test ical then dumb. Thepointis even . hoguhI don't have a job
an d I don't ha e enough success to get Terry Grossto be interested in how
I made a million dollars, I do have the good sense to have been born in a first
world country and als I'm fairly goodlooking though the m ans lessandless.
Fine. Let's talk about you, Reader. You like manda in orange La Croix club
soza in an illuminum ca n from your frostry refrigerator. You have repla ced
the lightbulb in your fresh food section with a blue light. You can recognize
when a household issu hasbeen handledwith duct tape. You don't get weepy
whayou have to pick up what you had neve reven considered until nowto be a mess.
You like Hondas. You know when you get to nothing but Raisn Bran in the morning
it doesn 't necessarily mean it's time fo groceries. You like the collage
ofthe family inDublin. You like S even Daedelus . Somehow for some reason you
have this awes me abiltiy to pick out the most tasteful drawer pulls .

You take Prozac. You are a memb rof the Prozac nation. Yourson has a friend nmedZack. It is5:15 in the pm. You h aveyour health. You are thinkijng well andinspired but not that inspired. So you liketoys that work with magnets.

Dear Diary, This morni g I skimmdthe local a ts m gazine. I t was filled with the vibraboy of a city tryingto redifineitself. Rober Pinsky says he don't like rap but then he hasn't exactly investigaed it asthouroughly as hewoul liek to but he knows that if he did he would find that most of it is b d and ver bad and derivitive but he knew she would als very likel y find much tha he did respect a dadmireandwel l LIKE. Actually, tha's only a rough approxima tionof ehat he said. I hear d a critic say oncethat Chri tian rock isthe only musical genreb inwhicbrilliance is impossible.

Dear Diary, fr m today on Iam go°ng to never ev r credit o anything I think Isworth repeaing and a s penance for this I will also never sg t e what I say is something I believein. If you knew me, dear Di ry you would realize t hat this is not tha bif a step for me anywa, given my enthusiasm for IDEAS . BTW, id fomeone tells you that you are awesome becalseyou hav so matny great ideas yod shou ld punch them in thefac e so tha they fall into the gutter with out even liftingtheir handsin frontof their face to buffer t e fall. If I lift my arm, if I say I a m raising my arm,tha t is a ver differ rent thi ngthan saying my arm lifts up. Ever y se tiem being id a kingdom withina burrito. And a burrit i s a penis and a taco i a female sex organ.

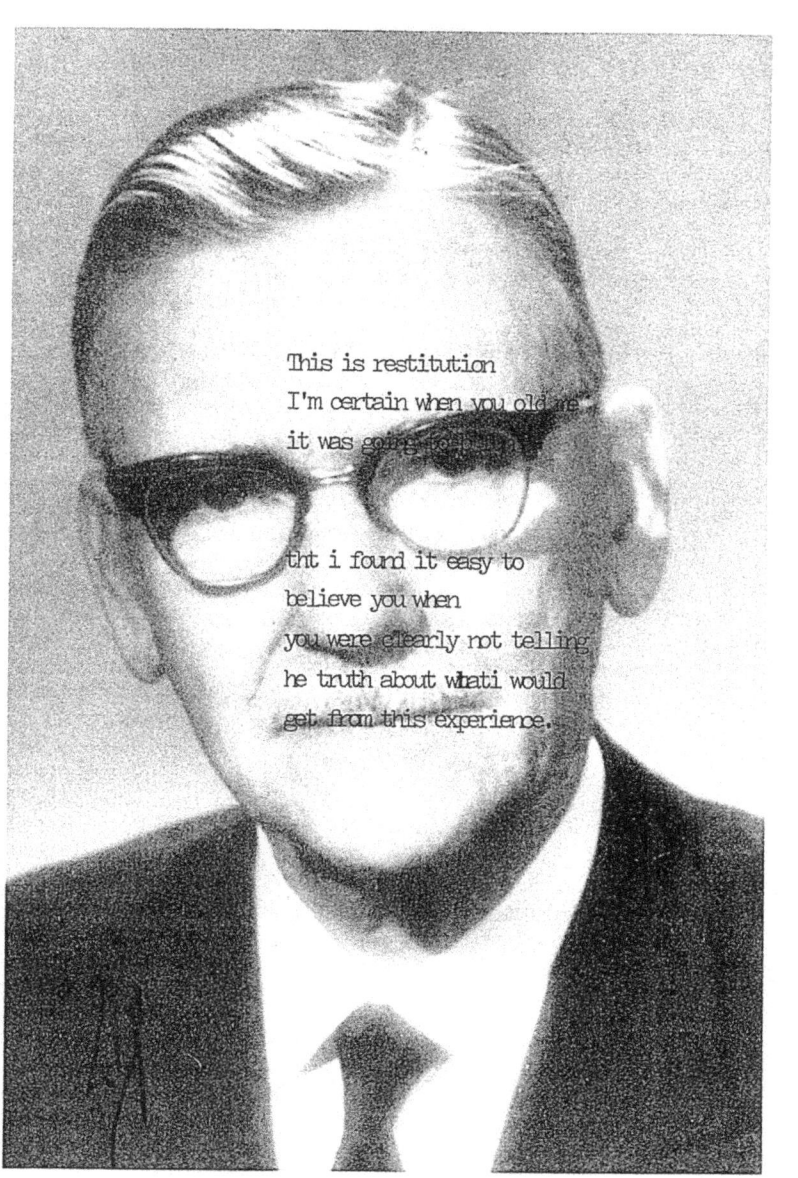

The first step to changing your life is to brush your teeth with an electric tooth brus h.
2nd step.: Gather up all the unlit tealight candle s scattered aroun athe house ana put them in a sandwich ba g.
3rd step: Tell her your th one she's dreaming of --
4th step· Aske her out a:;dtreat h rli₿ a lady.
5th step: Tu;n your smartphone b ck on.
6th steo: Make a to do/ to don't list.
7th step: If you are socially stupid or / lonely share your sta us on my butt.
8th step: Don't tell the story of how the birth of your chilfren was like a train wreck, was like being the observer of a trainwreck i tha t is sure y my butt.
9th step: Be happy and say to yourself you are happy and becaı se you hv e yor heal t: and the illuʂon of safety andshelteɛ an· the loveof ana. resp ct of your children an a couple of friends you have all m you need to be happy.
10th step: Learn, try to leʀn how to understand the live the 9th step wiṭ out having to hear it from someone else especiàly at churc or at school or wor k or t teas. For we're ₇ll of us Saints of God and I m an I ',m hpoing to b eone too.
11th step: (Partly wh t sustains me -oh it's been such   longjourney (: is knowing th t what I,m writɧ is real. It's cloudless. It takesthe b st of whaṭ technology hasto offer muct: like a rocket stove fo camping and trablatesit into keystroke s and ink and the whole thing beng this thing that's not epheneral.)
12th step: Do w hat the new nice pope sɟ sandhelp otrers. Think of others this y ear/time more ha n you th ink of yourself.
13th step: Learn how to make a number I on a manual typewriter :I1L1. It8s a lowercae "1#". Duh.
14th step: Listen to liberal , public radio programs.
15th Step: Make a   snothi e with milk, ice, greek yogurt, raisin bran, cat food, frozen blueberries, peanut butter, ana love.

16t step: Woody Allen used the same typewriter, ha , used ,uses the sametypewriter he usedw ehe bought it in 12953.
So the 16th step is to hte Woody Allen because he is a pedophile and a mysogonist andis unapologetic an cansomehow get awy with telling Murie l Hemingwa tht he is beautiful byading war adpeace while he sh oct sa movie all arounf her becasue she isth& cool . Later she would commit suicide. Actua ly i,m not sure about that . Either sh ecommittedsuicideor he married a healthy guy in California who helpedh r chngeher life by doing yoga andspeedngdown thecalifirni free w on their wy to a boulder at sunri se in whic this reporter couldnot hap butnotice his irritationat h er thetraffic. Comeon,Honey. we aregoingt miss it.Only squares wear shoes. Did you knowt ahalf the nutritionyou get from smoothiescom sfromt. bottomsofyour feet. Y eop t t 's right, you just suck thas sh it up thro ough your corns andt e cracksbetween y our toes. Whydo you think God gav eus fungus ? Why indeed.

I'm judging you because you
 are judging me
ndif i get there first then I win
the war

I will call you
when you are alone
in the room
of my eyes

when i am alone in the room
allI am are eyes
oceans and oceans
of eyes
I see you
when i
we are in

If I come outof this ituation I am goingto be very relieved.
Once I am free from these integumins, I shall be very.
Later, I will be even more happy.
The reason I will behappy is because I will have accomplished something
I have long resoected as a very ritgeous quality in others. Like Jay-Z
for instance. It goespore, pose, pose. So just to reiterate and since
this is what I got and that might not be a lot. I just want to say
that I knowthe sentence before thisone was a runon into by buttjuice
is too strong. All this, let it beknown funeralperson th at all ye
witness upon here is the happy truth.
Con sciscion.
I wabt this to be a story. And I want it to go on for a while and want
it to have enough energy to mke it beyonf the pale of the premise
So now I'm going to try to be less meta frank's arm islifting yet he is
not liftingit. I'm goingto tell a story. One that's goingto take from
you-know conversations an mash them all up. But before that and at t
herisk of sounding Jay-Z only you-know, how many pageswould I haveto
write oft his quality to make th is meditatio ala Montaigne wotth
some th ing.

In heaven you don't need no glasses.
Who would havethought that Bret Easton Ellis had so much to teach me.
Thanks, Bret. Tell Kanye and Marilyn and Kev and Judd I said yo yo yo.
I was goingto write a story when i stoppe dlast night.
I was going but then I wemt. Tod ay I told my students that theyr are
dumb. But in away that would challenge them to try to be smart and
smarter than me.   If he cou uld only b eajk freefrom the excellent
          entertainment onth internets
Brett "Easton Ellis is going it alone.
Brett Easton Ellis has a bit of a cold.

Brett Easton Ellis worries that some people won't understand.
Brett Easton Ellis does NOT worry that some people won't understand.
Brett Easton Ellis has an agenda.
Brett Easton Ellis answers his Twitter feed audibly.
Brett Easton Ellis believes that Audible . com is a n endorseable website.
Brett Easton Ellis has a bit of a vold.
Brett Easton Ellis answers emails before he writes until 6 or 7 pm andthen it is cocktail hour.
Brett Easton Ellisw would want me to say I should hire someone to say, Wlecome to the fg pod cast.
Bret Easton Ellis frank william gampetra
Frank Weathers Giampo workshard to print a thing with one tom of rules.
The ghost of Bret Easton Ellis opeadth cover of my RCYAL. Ne could be Royal, sgs the ghost.
Brett Easton Ellis isra remrkable perdonality in hat there are times whe I hate him andhis ent ire range of emotions are because he is both stupid and boastfull.
Brett Easton Ellis is goingto grow even old er with me. If he ism lucky.
Brett Easton Ellisiswilling to toot hisown horn. Like
Brett Easton Ellis thisproject
I am as committed to completeing
I am am to continuing to do a
7 minute workout. every day beczusd its short.
Brett East n Ellis says youngwriters should make some noiseon 19ne.

Brett Easton Ellis would make me very nervous to tzlk to in a way that would makehim bored with me. Even if I were prepared.

(inverted text:)

To An Older Lover

Alone, I start to forget how not loving you feels. With you, our two hearts struggling in their cavities, falling. Please heal soon, so I can leave you. I've never been less happy. But without you, this mountain range seems so dark, all I feel is fear. off the mountains; that bright sound of constant should break apart and course down It should be spring by now. The streams I hope, while tissue mends around the stents. and ruin the wiring. You're an hour north, asleep, in the walls I'm still awake, staring into blank and listening cover these woods so covered by the Catskills. lawn, the brittle humus and bramble. Shadows quiet, and shadows edging over the frozen March night. From the mountains, a heavy

24

If you left your house and you wnet to buy some apples at Whole
foofds and you got yourself into a car wreck ata an interesection
as chance would haveyou do, what porn would you have found in your home?
What horde, Beowulf? Edwacker?

My naeis Eadwacker and thisis the story of how I wound up at Hades
High school.
--Who her? That/s my hs sweetheart. Her skin is small.
I am a whaler by trade. My father was one. I am from the same family.
Your hero who divesdown the farthest without a tank, wit only
theweight , hewould sgoot purposelessly off the horizon jus t asyou
would if you were onewho was not buckledto the earth by a building
or a wall or resing against a cliff. All the pretty girls call me Ed.
Oh Ed how do you do it th is? andoh Ed how do you keep a thought together
on Aderal that .
Thenew Ap 7 Minute Workout Challenge avail ble to down oadthrog h theap
storeby Fitness Guide Inc in t e Hea thandfirnesscategory snox ap.
I used it. Today.
Good musi c good anyth ig is just you can't think of anything dumb
or bad while you are experiencing it. No. You can't think of anything
outsi eof it. Can' t loook at t e face of anyonewho would not choose it,
who w uld not change stakons or ASK HER ADULT DAUGHTER TO please
turn itoff. I'm th inking Bret Easton Ellis loves him some Bdck.
He's all like Beck said this and Beck said that .
What id thekey to being talent d at something, world class talented
is tha y ou are lucky en oug to happen on the meduim that most
quickly putsyour most sincer th oughts on thepage.
I shall now write a story for each member of my family. As a kind
ofstory, for every single member of my family.
Eadwacker's Tale
 (to becontunued)

Badwacker's Tale

for Hula and Caruso andakl the other pets these old bones haveknown

Se--h-a-i---ae-ve-at-ays---t-Pr-

It's been a while,Love. And an even longer while since we ate cinnimon toast.
New nail polish on my thumb pulls on the nail an makesme aware of my nail. This is bad andsomething that is bad.
My mom keeps sending me newspaper articlesabout up and coming poets livingin Houston, Texas. She send them in envelopes that are already addressed to businesses andindividuals who might beinterested in using the servicesoffered by the appliancebusiness I us d to manage with my father from 1994 until 2006. You can tell, if you are interested in telling, t t it's been a while since I last typedon this machine because I've forgotten where to find the numberone key. I will find it no w: iIlL   llllll 12 23 1969. There it is , th4 lwer case 1. Thelonely unheralded lower case 1.
This morni g I woke up to discover that that I hadmissed the scheduled pick-up of a rug tha my sister sent me but wasn't supposed to send me becauseh rstep daughters wanted to have it. They b oth have babies. Onehasa ba y and a medium-small dog. I wanta MaineCoon cat but I can't justify buying a pet whe there are so many pets in so many shelters that need a home. Whn I went back to sleep thismorning after my discovery of missngthe pick-up, I dreamedth recurringdream of my wife not wanting me to comehome anymore. It felt so real because it was an issue that she was- h d comfortably left at the back of her mind. Neh, had comforta bly forgotten was an issue at all. It gaveher s senseof breeziness unlike my. Whereas my state of mind was troubled, but asusual. So we would talk a d interact as if everythin was the sam asit always is only to bereminded of thefact that I was thankfully to her notliving wit h ror did not haveto go homewith her this day and so she was relieved. So then I had to be more patient an and morein control ofmy emotion s which hasnever been a strong character trait of mine but tnen who am I comparing myslef to. As i lezrned whe I delivered appliancesfor my father's appliance buness, most people live way morelike animals than t the do like angels. Andeven the people who have houses that are clean enough for angelz to eat off the bathroom floor, they have furnishings and colors and knick knacks tht an amphibian brain would refuse to lie on ev n lft ese thingswere bat e din Arizona sunlihgt. (now I am getting all lyrical.) My wife didn't need me in this dream. Well, she needed m me but she didn't need me dribbling my middleage manpee on the floor of her very clean bathroom. So in the dream I was desperate and scared and well unmoored. Turnd out that it takes me a couple ofdays to get use d to being ina different location. This whole drive to Mairo this , then dri ve to Clevelrnd Heights thing. It's hard. VS Naipaul says oneshould not be ableto fly froma third world country to a first world country becauseit's toormuch of a psychicshock. When I got back to my place in Cleveland Heights this time I made myself a dinnr with spinach I had purchased beforeI left. h plastic rectangular box said do not use after January 22nd. I read this on January 32st. The day after I cook e a dinne rof tofu, garlic, onions, balsamic vinegar andof course lots of spinach. Three timesis the numberoftimes I found myself sittn in frontof my toilet. And each of th ose three tim s I wretched three times an threw up so much. Thenumber 6 is suppoed

a perfect number because you can add its divisors and still get the number 6. 6&6&6- 1&2&3-6 Maybe I8m thinkingthisi the perfect medium for little old me becauseI don't have to promoteit or share it or editit or wonder ifanyone will read it becuase I know they won't66- Well, Iknowthey won't 99% of th way to 100%. But yet I'm writing and I'm doingsomething that requires enough effortthat I can't fall asleep while I8m doingit. Which is the problem,or, will betheproblem whsone can just think a t ought and th thought will be recorede andpe ple will think Oh boy even thogh I can't type or write or communicate ver well with a yoneincluding my life partner , I can write a novel. I can tink a novel. No you can't. Andyou can't paint andyou can't coach football, andyou can't be a good radio host for NPR andyou can' build a one flor office in your backyard, andyou can't be a prek teacher and you can't be a guy a who spreadsmsalt on the roadsin the winter. You can't do anything that on first investigationlooks easy or requires a skill set that seems vlose to your own. Wht is our skill set , anyway? Mine is that I am the b st guy in t he whole world. How did I lean this skill? By not running away from home as a child. By persevering through child hood in the samehouse wher e I was m de warm and given love and respect andsometim es admiration. 99% of who we are is invisibleto us. 99% of who I am is invisibleto me. This meansthat nabove all, I am not ab;e to experience the 99% of situations in lifewhere there's a question abou t howI would react to it. "Handgrenade in the foxhole, fg? you andyour son in the gas chamber deciding who gets the moldy spinach bread crust from Dagostinos,fg? The ladyy who told the kid that she has problems too , who told thekid who cameinto the junior highschool to signhimselg in while we aring a hoody and a carrying comfortablty andwith confidenc s flame throwerlearned that she was a hero. She learned this by listenignto the 911 call she had made whe he came in. She said she thought she was screamin:inside. Thesaid she hadjust received the neww that her car was being repossessed andshe would ha eno way to come to work at the school the next day. That's wha thiz white boy dressed in black came into theoffi e with his flame thrower to sign i n because he was late. At my daughter's school th y hav ea camera outsixe the front d oorsandyou hav eshow your face to it and if the know your faceorlike your face or your facedoesb'tlook too mad they will let you in. Thy will buzz you in. Thogh it doesb't really buzz. It all takes pl ce in silence. ooooooh. Silence. My iphone is ajing meifI have 7 minute tes t o spare to do a 7 minute workout. Whenever I do a workout I notice that I am always a little surprisee by how mycg pain hurts. Note to self: pain hurts.

The man did not want to die. So he made sure to keep his phone with him wherever he went in the hosse that nigh. He was alone. In his rented house in "Cleveland Heights. If he died none would find his body for a minimum of 24 hors and more likely more than that. But that's not why he so desparately wanted to live. No. He wanted to live becasue he did not want his children nor his wife to have to tell the story od how their father/husband had decided whether were young all d one in a house in Cleveland Heights. Cleveland? the would say? No my faher didn't livr in Cleveland. He just worked there. He lived in a suburb that was slightly elevated and southeast of the city called Clevelabd Height s. The rea lestate there is so cheap you can rent a nice home to a whire boy tryingto make a living in the arts. Thom Yorke said I am do lucky and when he did Alec Baldwin cut him off. Alec Baldwin kept immitating Tom Yorke's accent. It was terrible and made more terrible because of the medium of radio, of audio only. Pound syas you shouldn't give advice to a writer if younyourself haven't written a great work ofwriting.

Pound was a fascist. Fascists sometime smke goodwriters and orators.

Here is what I know: This time I'm not working with an engineer or a producer. This time I'm going to learn it all via Lynda.com. This time I'm going to do all my shopping at Walmart. This time I'm going to keep an xml doc that shows the prices for the 13 items I buy most. This time I'm going to take out $100 and that cash is going to have last the whole week. If I want a beer at a bar on Thursday and all I got is not enough then I go give somebody a blowjob and make sure nobody tries to give me the good guy discount. The good guy discount is what my friend Dan says he wants to try. As "hey I'm a good guy, right? And you are a good guy, right? So how about giving me a good guy discount on these *****?? Studies show that 8 out of 10 cashiers will say no. But you have to ask all 10 to figure out who is the good guy. Is this why you would ask me for something? Dear Diary, I just got a damn text from a damn person who wants something from me and that's okay because n I'm a goodguy after all but this person is taking up brain space that could be filled with important thoughts about myself. Why don't I show up 15 minutes early for myself? I knew the answer to this qiestion before I got yhe fucking text from the fuckingperson who fucking wants somethig from me. That's for sure. Screw this whole bla bla bla bla and bla.

Once upon a time there was a man who was 99% invisible to himself and most all others. And all the others were the 20% who would give anyone who asked a good guy discount but you have to ask is all. Anyway, the following is the story of Bret Easton Ellis's life. Ten thousand hours are the number of hours it takes to, learn how to make a really good fortune cookie. BTW, why is it that you have to help a chef do a demo? Can't I just watch and imagine I6m there?
This is a problem with typing. The problem is this. I feel like I'm thinkin-lots less interesting thoughts because I have to be so concerned with the damn typing. Dan is going to bring me an arcgival box to store all

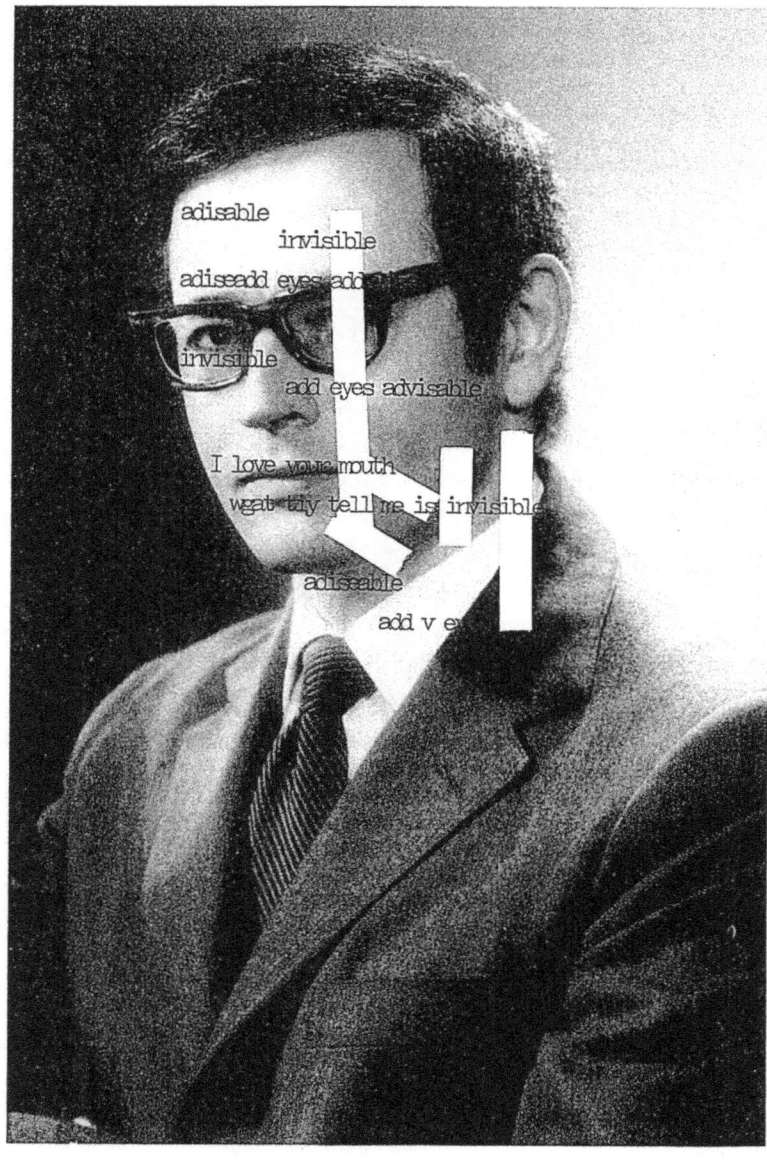

these pages in. What a nice guy.

So Heather and I were wearing our head scarves andlookingdown into the ravinethat ran through the Jordan Valley andwere were just sitting there on our hotel blankets when these two small girls cameup to us and askedus to teach them English. The n they both say down on our blankets i with usand oneofthem picked up a rock. She smashed the rock and then spat spat on the center mos t portionofthe stone abd then zhe dug out the centerwith herthumbnail andshe put tha bit ofrock in my palm and she spat ij my hand. My friend said , my frie ndHeathr said OOOOh gross. Thegirl sittingnext to herxaid oooooh gross. My little friend rubbed her spit into therock she hadjus given me andrubbed and rubbed kind of like a shiatsu person. Ajd as she rubbe dthe paste turned blue. We , Heather and I said, Whoa, that's mest up andweird. Do you thinkit's okay. andte girls said oh they are talking at the same time as if they a e oneperson, just as we do. Then the onewho expectorated into my handaske dme to closemy eyes using sign la guage. Andwhen I did she s smeered the blue rock paste onto my eyelids abd into my cheekes andalso a little on my lips. Wow. Now.

fg csnnotsustain tension over longstretchexof time.
fg cannot sustain tensoin in anything heiswriti'ng unless it is very short
fg cannot sustain tension in a short story about women.
fg cannotsustain tension because the depths ofhisself loathing are
deep andwide. asifthey were.
fg sometine sgets lucky butnotlucky e ough to not feel miserab le bout
all theth ing she is nit doingbyt should bedoing.
fg cannotsustain tension with anyn medium that would or could
makehim a buck.
fg wantsnoth ing to do with thinking tha maeskesm him think andthink
andwantAmbien to . Xanex doesnot'ing for fg. Someone els eha salready
written a novel caled "TheDrug Book"

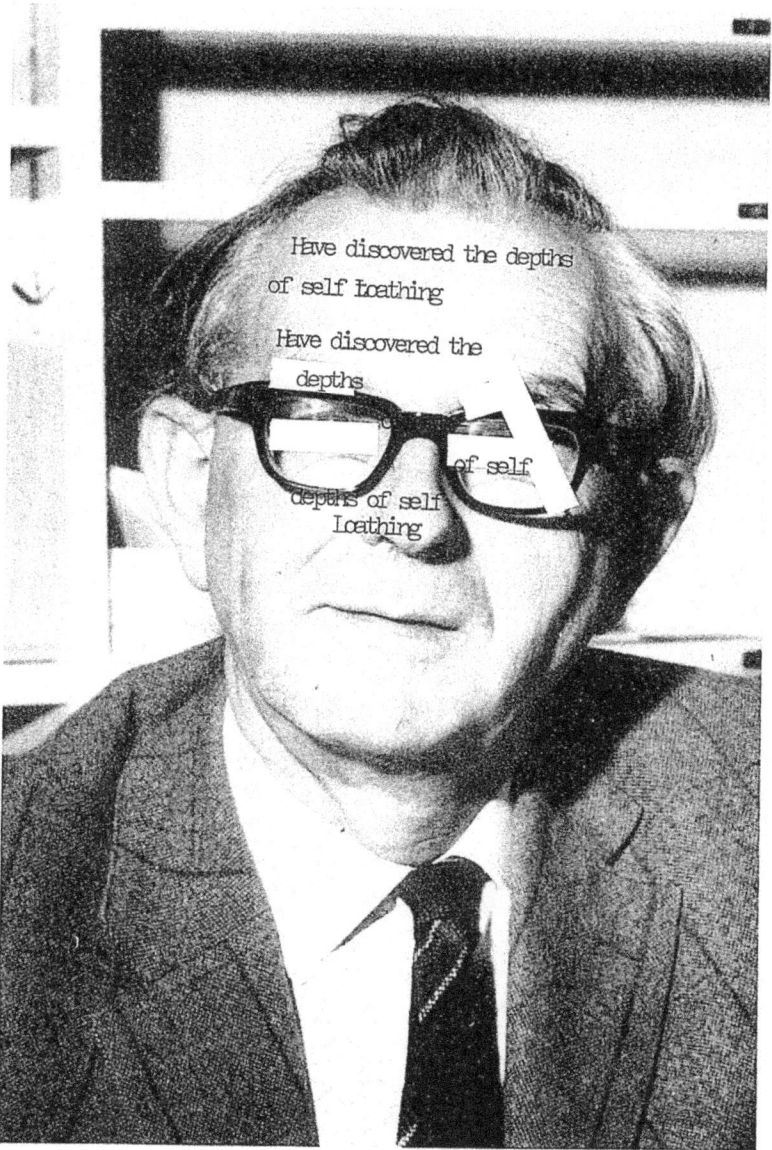

Jeff Garlin seems like a nice guy. He doesn't have "no regrets."
But he does have some regrets, a handfull of rgretts. Phillip
seymoure Hoffman died today. The super bowl is today. I spemnt too
much money at Whole ?Foods today. And i did not spendany time with my
kids today. Th ey are surely suffering: becauseof this, but at least
I am al ive. Phillip Seymour Hoffman always had the look of someone
who washiding something whenever I saw him in character, but then
I only reakized this just today s nce hearing about h9s death.
I think I may be listening to too many podcasys that feaure famous people
talking about themsleves in a way that makes them seem approachable
and like their success is likemy success if I were a success. Maybe
I shouldtake a class in stand up comedy since I am living in a place
wherethey teach stand up . Maybe then I could get my own TV special.
Maybe then I could sustain myslef while d ingsomethigI love and is insp i
ringt others. Wha t if I just call d my kids and dedicated my time
to soending really and truly interesting times with them. we could
ma e a 30 second horror film andupload it to YouTube an d Wes Craven
couldviewit andwe woulwin a bigprixe. If I don't figute out a way to
make money doingwhat I love then my children will not be able to figure
out a way to mke money doingwha thy love. Tht , dear Reader is the
American dream for self-serving solypsictical arts fartsy intellectual
typessuch as myself. I wea shoes . My fahe r wore cloggs. My bhildren
will wear cloggs. Of course this is nottrue. Actually in the early 90s
I ha s n awesok pair of black cloggs. There8s a pictu re of meso mewhere
wearingthe cloggs andandboxer briefs and smoking a cigarette on my back
deck of thehouse& where I usedto live Dover, Delaware. So, Donald Revel
says a poem is a little machine for creativereading. It's a something
you ca read in order to interestingl y experiencetheminutia that stays
news. Pound the fascist says lotsofthings . Jeff Garlin is a nice gu7
and famous and al l tha but if I couldn'tee eat cheese and hadto get accupu
   ncture and take vitaminsand search for balance I would just not do anyth

34

I had a friend namedLarry ewho hada script. dor Adde½altm).
He did 90mg eachday . Wait , hed id 20 mg three tim sa day.
Well that's what h was suppOsed to do. Butinstaed he would very often
do 80 mg a day. This ment tht toward the end ofevery m ont: he got depe
essed becausefor ev ry day t a hedid 80 instead of 60 he hadto do 40
Pointis , t istook up a lot ofhisthinkingandisprobæly a lot of what
took up a lot of Phillip Seymour Hoffman's thinking even though he
was a wildly successful artist andvery well respected bynlotsofvery smrt
people. Anywa, Larry did this routine month after month after mont unt.
il low andbehold one day hediesd ort he world came to an endottherewas
not morepharmacies because someonehad destroyedthe financia system with
a cyber virus and hefeltpretty bad for a couple ofweeksbut then he
gotbetterbecauseall aroundhimwas devastation andhoror andpeople way
worseoffthan he was . So he lived andhe met his family inPalm ?Sprinsgs
Californi˛ whic h is still lovely even ifyou can'tget money outofa
n atm machine. Andt e found a houseandt˛g kille dthepeople who were
living it andthe housewas great becauseit had a palm spring in the
back yard . Well tht was thelifeame thefurniturewaseven fairly nice.
For some reason noonewas in Palm Sprirg seccept the cgildren of Jeff
G'arlih. Well Larry took ten in becauseJeff Garlin dieddurin;tne
aftermath ofthe financia upheavel tht ensuedafe r thevirus made
everyones' bank bhance go t zero. Hiskidswere okg . --I guess I am
just sorep cause J eff Garlin would have is all think that
ifyou a e niceand you say nice thins about people andthe y agree
that you arenicether you will become successful andfamous. I for one
do not believe this. There. Call me cynical. Call meexactly what I shoul
d expect given my exper erpesand situatu ionherein exile in Cleveland
but that's wha 1 think. Which is influencedin no smal l part to the
mechnicsofhaving to push down so forcefully on these keys to mkean y
kind of thought TAT ALL. By t ewæy , Bells Two Hearted Ale, in the
 year 2014 ofourLord is a very d amn good beer. NowLarry hasto go
   be nice to himself. Which is to say heha to find a job at an than

collections. Now that's a racket where it doesn' pay to be nice. That's a racket where you've got to be interested in the idea of pre emptive striking especially if you have a house in Palm Sprins and the money system has not collapsed and The Facebook is still a good place to put your money.

The NPR Internist Makes A Big Mistake

It was a Sunday night and Larry was yelling at me to find a clip of Phillip Seymour Hoffman in Death of a Sale sman. So I scanned the fi fib z s for the same and found the following : Willy Lowman an Biff Malcovich/Lowmann Biff Hoffman so I figured that's the one and als my timer was in there d. I haet is job. Every night I call my dad nd tell him e and while I'm on the phone w to hom I drink a can of Cherry coke. wib a starw , and BTW, no plastic. Right? Right. So I come to find out when I walk in to the studios on Monday tha it was Dustin Hiffman and well boy did I get an earfull. And tha night I couldn' t find and cherry coke in bottes and boy my old ma get an earfull. Tha t wws all a longt me ago when people used emá l for most of their communication now it's just smike signal tis and shout real loud if you see anyone trying to do a preemptive strike on our camp and small stotge of supplies . I'm just glad I'm not working at NPR anymore. Fuck the news. Fuck the won world. And Fuck tis n typewriter for being a loud and echoey in t ese here new growth soft wood woods. Hear the wind in tose needles, ?

I'm done. Seriously. Done.
Doneisntoostrong a word. I'm finished. A finisher. A guy who comesout on top, one who always seems to find a way. Sure I'm 90 and ugly butlook at this tie. Look at these shoes. Feel this leather. Feel it. Sometimes for like five minutes at a time I get so lonesome I want to die. But then I make my way down Cedar to Vespers at Saint Paul's andthen I'm off to thepoets house on Essex for seessex.

I Hauwe Have a Terrible Fear
after Cesar Valejo's "Tengo un miedo terrible."

I have a terrible fear that jazz music will play at 11pm.
I have a terrible fear that jazz music is music depresses me.
I have a terriblefear that motion sickness is a stimulant.
I have a terrible fear that I will comeup with another idea for having a terrible fear.
I have a terrible fear that my yellow 1 ball will get me killed in ww3.
I have a terrible fear that hips and low hills will my show don't tell.
I have a terriblefear that Poundis a fascist and everything he says about writing isright.
I have a terrible fear that sex is overrated until you're ratingit.
I have aterriblefear that this particular jazz station is killing me.
I hav a terriblefear that I will read this and rate each line.
I have a terriblefear that Deb is right and oneshld. never explain.
I have a terriblefear tha explaining is just apologizing light--lite.
I have a terrible fear that kids today are learning to code anfthat mean a I'm going to haveto go to Pisa for pizza with some snotty grand kid.
I have a terriblefear that one day my mother will die.
I have a terriblefear that I am no longer pretendingtobe a grown up.
I have a terrible fear that I am just a minor monster.
I have a terriblefear I am terrible becauseI keep thinking down to trese stupid stupid binaries.
Maybe it's this music.
I have aterriblefear that Robert Bly is a heluvagood defender.
I have a terriblefear that I don't need to talk shit about Robert Bly.
I have a terrible fear of any hammondorgan I am notin control of.
I have a terrible terrible fear.
 I hav a terribleterrible fear.

ThisisFranj Giampietro. Welcome to Don't tell, show" wherewe show you wgat's happening in writing, the arts, music, philosophy, neuro-philosphy DIY , Issuesof Privacy, neuro ethics psychology, and pedagogy, What ever it is w3 bringyou,wjtls show you what it's all about.

Maybeoneofthe first episodeswill be about how blind people understand the notion of show don't telland also come we'll hear somewacky stories about blindpeople being asked if they can see what you mean?

Dateline February 14th, 2014:
As the city slept the internet took away every privacy including the privacies where men who are growers not showers with long pubic hair are shown at the beginning and ending of each movie blockbuster.
A sort of "Let's All Go to the Lobby."
I8m the L Ron Hubbard of poetry.
I'm not joking. I'm the L Ron Hubbard of change the word from remember to imagine. I'm like all that shit is so dumb and I'm not really just trying to control you no more, I'm trying to control Wakim Phoenix which is.
Hairlip girlfriend , Happy Valentine's day. Hairlip sucker. If I had a hairlip girlfriend I would just commit to it.
I would say hey, Lenny. It's Saturday and you're at the red office and she's at the office. Recently, America I watched the film The Apartment. starring not Walter Mathow but the other guy Felix and also Sissy Spacek's mother only I know she's not urban, she's Montana country. The Russians are victims. That's what the intellectuals with Russian accents say. Tomorrow I leave for Italy where I will express myself on TV -Boobies as the passionate thinker I happen to be.
So if I were going to write about teaching poetry I would begin something like this:

I heart page 18. There so I said it and now I want to get back to our
story of how I ought to write some of this teaching down. Well, one
thing I know is once I taught 8th graders who were xmarter than most
other people in the city of Cleveland and beyond. Turns out lots of Canadians are extrememe conadians and that means them Russians better get.
So I tell them so me more about this teachers and how I had may teachers like th
that and it felt good am sometime x I would go to a class and sit there an
listen and it was just like going to the movies only the lights are flour
escen in most classrooms. Once recently a steam shovel hit the side of
the bui.dignin which I was teachin and when it did it woke up the
red haired bearded twenty something of the hobbit viking explain how
funny I am routine kid. And a hey image what image I'm wondering and
why do I get to teach the most well dressed writers in Ohio? Why indeed.
Dr. Depresso was Telemachus of a man, Dr. DePresso was a laurel crown
reminder, ad a brilliant nihilist, the mos brilliant. And his wife is very
upbeat. THERE were others, DD. Judith Roof, I would be boring you with
this, too. Point is one of the highest levels of learning is to be like
that, to beloving every minute you are in the presence of the teacher
and striving with 3 others to find a reason to stick around because
you want to stay in the dream. Suddenly I feel and sound feel I sound
like Donald Revell at the end of memoir on a lifetime of paying attention
called, "Attention". Or not. So you tell each one take a turn staying afte
r letting her vagina double or triple in size. NO NO NO. I know .
I just wanted to see what that felt like for a sec. Yuck.
This hig est level of learning chang s your brain, makes a many a wrinkle
and when get that Bplus you get it. The other highest level of learning
is to diametrically oppose your teacher at every step of the way. As in,
Oh you're all like privacy is a big deal well I saw a special on privacy
and it said you people should all jus go back to typing on a typewriter.

At the end of the day the scientist and the artist go home with stains.
So they can grow T-cells in a salinebrine . Saline -brine is redundant.
How come sometimes I can keep myself from thinking a dumb thought andthe next I hand the professor a paper on making platelettes in a briny
mixture. Cherie would tell me I've lost my thread. She is a friend
in the stoic sense of the word which is as if it were a stain. Today
a brown lightpole in aparkinglot broke my radiator .
I have a terrible fear that I will have some difficulty.
That your difficulty is my shelter. And my heater.
I have a fear of feedback. It's the surprise that tells what an ass
I would be in a foxhole. Oneday the scientist said he hadwritten a
novel about a man on Mars and how he survived and you are darn right
I did the math. I did all the math. Another day a scientist saidwe
are at the end of the beginning in termsof our understanding of Stem cells never mindplatelletes. Then anotherscientist said we have 4 kinds of
bias that we can't completely explain and then anoter scientist was all
like big data in hour butt, bigdata in your butt! Then therewasthe
scientist who waslike where is all thedamn antimatter? It's like there
should be way way more. So oneday they made LHC Large hadron? Collider
that went all the way around the world at sort of a diagonal andthat
one, it turnedout wasbig enough. Poof I.
I have z fear that the heater will comeon.
Andmost of all right now recollected in tranquility I have a terrible
fea that my right ear is throbbing with a dull sharp low pain and it
means I'm crazy lulu migrainey andor --Theheater just kicked on.
Today Cherie said to Daphne, Hey, look at the cows, Daphne. But they
the thing Cherie saw wasn't cows. It was a pile oftires in the deep
snow of thewinter of '14. (Just realized that thisvey Nicholson Bakery
thiswholeonepieceof paper a dsy record rumination la lla . Good night
mandwith first name of Nicholson. Goodnight.

In Which the Writer Learns to write while turning

In which the mermase maces the mew.
In which German measles are colonized.
In which the whole foods bot jumpedup and down
bagging my frozen pizzas giving back correct cange like had been doing t
his whole life which only just begunblike two years ago. I told him Yeah,
see the whole world is after you and you can't tell itbutthat's what
that's what in which the man wrote his first 4 bodice rippers.
I would rather not write than write a love affair with a misgendered
season, or like death w/ a capital DDD.
Tonig t is no good. I'm no good. The schools are nof good and if you
cant't see that well then you're blind to tthe stars coming down on the
tall deep grass which also contains a certaindoppelganger's shadow.
Peter had Wendy sew his on. Losigg your shadow would be like chapping
your felt green kYin. Like your mind was chapped, like you got a burn.
Do i like my Bose headphones, peope on theinternets? Uniquivocally,
I may state tht they are worht the $339.99 ± spent.--Not 339".
$239.99. That's what thy cost like 5 years ago when I bought then
when ± hadsome money to buy the best , Baby. Once, Baby,± bought and
owned a Porsche, a sports car, rifing with the window down. That was
me. That was me also who couldn't get the window to roll back up.
The boystonguewas made lik a sheet of hot glass ij that in the summer
his tongue shijed lik theswordsof the angels starigg at Adam and Eve
as they walke dand talked. They had a conversation just like you and Adam
do, Erin. Please promote my to-do. You are marketing wonderfulness.
Dear LordJordan, play your harmonica and if agthing really bad ever happ
ens to me and JerryJordan Lord knows it will. Not now. Though. Noyyet.
Not on Moracah almonds. Moracan amondseaten outofan ass wit Nutella
and bacon and mayo for my fries, BayBee. Doo doo doo-ooo do-o-oooo.

At thistimof day one can find a lot feel is wrong with the planets
and the 25k mile wide stormalways on the horizon of Jupiter for ex.
But that,s not what love is, Jenny. I know what love is.
It's May and it's 2014. And posterity is dead. So is memory. For me
and my family, anyway. He said , his Lezzbian wicken eye falling
slifing, siftingdown his thick middle finger other wise knownas
a bird especially known as a bird by the poet's daughter who greets
him this way. Like a bird. Like a bird pooping from a hispeed
internet cable line. Like an old mouse with young blood.
Sblood is what a Shagespeare will call it. Sbloodis Macbeth would
wade-through, at first. Readyour Tarkovsky, Boy. Report!
Half-heartedly the man drew his curtains over his yellow room.
Half-heartedly, the man fed the birch bark into the typewriter.
Half-heartedly, he agreed with his wife about the eggs, the floors,
                  the schedule for the summer, the baslet of baskets,
                  the reason for the late spring, therain, more rain,
                  and tha the lack of bugs morethan makesup for this
                  feeling. It comes. It goes.

Here I wasthinkijgthat candorwasthis big deal because theguy
who cofounded Pixar says itis the I find out from Phillip Lopatetht
candoris a performance , at leas for writers. Andnotonly tht but
Lopate sy she's a ver provate guy andtht Montaigne said that not only
is candor a performanc e for the writer butso is intimacy . to which
I sa yes, sureall so if you can get a mother fuckerto read what you've
performed.

Gin Fizz
❊❊❊❊❊❊❊❊
fill a cocktail shaker with ice.
Add I ounce lemon juice.
L teaspoon sugar (preferably superfine)
and 2 ounces London Dry-style gin.
Shake vigorously and strain into a high ball glass.
Top with club soda.
Garnish with a lemon wedge.
Makes 1 drink.

Gin Mule
❊❊❊❊❊❊P❊
Fill a highball glasswith ice.
Add a scant teaspoon simple syrup, i 1/2 ouncesgin, 1/2 half ouncelemon juice and chilledginger beer to top.
Stir gently.
Garnish with a lemon twist.
Makesone drink.

               from what-are-you-drinking.html#drink/gin-mule
                                         gin-fizz

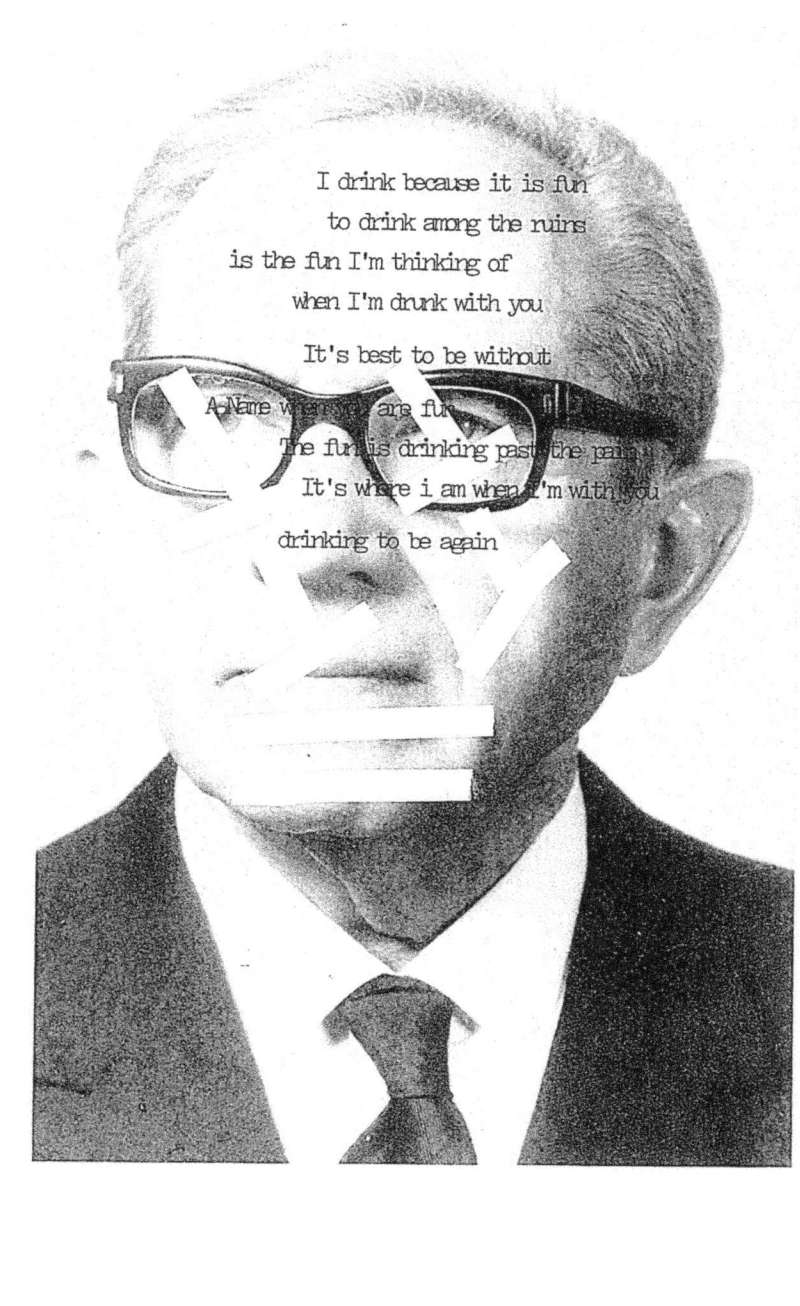

I keep finding really very nice furniture on the streets of this city.
I have a terriblefear that they have been pissed upon.
I have a terriblefear that I will live aslong as Beck ? Hanson and
never feel like he gets to feel. The movie I wouldHAVE to make isthe
onewhereBeck Hanson and Thom Yorke are bank robbers and the Brady
bunch are there. AndJan islike Cindy, cindy, blowjob.
I have a terriblefear that I am happy and there's no damn tensionin
happiness. Just ask Garriga Von Michael. It's too much work tobe careful
I ahave a terriblefear that I will never see the snow coming for my
knees as I memorize the course. I see mk KK-nees chattering bespoke-
for. I have a terriblefear that I may neverfeel what Steven Merritt has
felt. I have a terriblefear that I will neverfeel what it must feel like
to be John Travo.ta and be like Hey ?I have my own airportin my back
california yard. I have , a terriblefea tht it's not all that weirdtha
t the clock says 11:11.

Intellectual Jokes

Joke#1: A prisoner and a freeman are in a prison but the freeman/jailer is locked in the cell and the convict is on the outside and he's got a big club and latex in his breast pocket.

Hot summer night, windows are open, North Carolina pines and stones all around, and I am with my friend Julian and I am jerking off and showing him--him, him and me. And Robert Plant is singing thst down on my knees tbing. I've got to make more connections and do this whe I'm a little more me. I'm typing like I keep house. I'm thinking like I kep house, curriculum vitae. It8s 25.4 minutes from home to work. Sorry. Present. Sorry, Future. Nice to not be sorr for the past. F u, past.

Hey, Frank.
Is this the end of a beginning that works?
If all my cups [Beer glasses] were chilled, if every single one were chilled,
I would not be more corrupt. nor less likely
~~And now was one of~~ to search youtube to find a ~~video~~ 101 on how to
apply eye-liner.
~~I'm~~ going to be beautiful!
This is

The problem with problems is you never know when your blank is
going to have one. Oh. Is dinner ready? Nice and warm? Well here's
a
  na‾kin and here's a problem. This is why I never liked writing
because it's ask's me too slowly to think whilest I think.
poetry of stuff . . .
I got your stuff
is a

The problem just like ping pong is once you get stuck you get stuck. The mosquitos arrive,. They bring a peperroni and a bottle of wine. They are late. They are always late and never invite and drink blood and buzz in yourear (not necessarilyninnthat order). I like listening to Red SoxnBaseball . But the commercials make me wish I were dead. Whichn means I'm awefully affected. Am liable to be influenced. Stand for nothing. Fall for your butt. Which won't appologize for anything anymore. I&m still aliven , Jim Spangler. Are you? The hummingbird garden ornament floats above my workspace which is in the clouds which are in your butt if you live on Uranus. I say this , th4se those because it's the littlest thing I canado and still want to be here atall. Once I had the zing enough to want to be Bergman's butt. But that was a long time ago when we lived in the cabin on the hill. In the woods. Theze that I,think I know. Sometimesyountype. Sometimes you type faster and some times you
    stop typing and instead take a shower. Dear God, Today I e fixed the fan in the upstairs bathroom. Please when I haveto go and know i will go just as everyone ever did and does just like there are more dead people than living ones and etc., please let me in.
your humble etc.,

Last night I painted eyeballs on each oje or myfingernails, on my
left hand. Today I am using protein-enriched nailpolish remover
to clean my shotgun.
The only way i would ever own a shotgun is if my uncle Ray gaveme
oneof his. Then I would usegun cleaner to clean it but not as often
as as I would clean my bathroom if I livedalone. How can I be
som sure? How could Montale be so certain his servants were working
hard for him whilest hereadthe authors of antiquity? so deeply?
Thisisnpage 23,uLord. Andnow I must go out into the front yard and
mulch the ivy that has suddenly appeared and not been seen ijn
this part of Maine since 1973. Which is also the last time they used
giant concrete roller machine trucks to smooshnthedeep snow as it
fell. Back then. I saw anpicture. The averageperon in Americatales
1,000 pictures a year. That's 33.333333 images a day. Only when
you say the word images you are supposed to say "make" as in
the average person makes33.3333 imagesper day. Concrete chunks is
annimage i continue to return to . They saynthats all that will be
left of anything having to with humans making "making" anything
once we are all dead from the great war between the tiny -many
and the large-less many. 12 wars or fewer, not 12 wars or less.
I like to usethe word "elide" when I mean "remove"uwhen I'm speaking
to someone who wantsmy help. It takrs the stingout. I have a a tiny
growth on myn arm that is I think Cancerous. I am a Cancer but just

barely . By one day. One day. I will haveti die from something.
Brief list of things I do not wantto die from: falling chunks of
concrete, a canceroussoreon my left bicep caused bybprotein enriched
nail polish.

How many timez will haveto sweepmout the garage, Lord?
How many timewdo I get to sweep out the garage, Lord?
How many times
The cat is fritzed-out.
I am fritzed-out.
My son asked .e .f he couldminterview me.
Like any good pops i said yeah. Sure.m And also I says,
you can use your Google Voice to transcribe whatti says.
to which I says, So we do but nwe use pagesane the pagesuses Apple
Mac tim4s 10 which aint as good as google at least on the mobile
os , we'reb e weare talkijg about like OSX, Yo. Oh and OS 8?
Anyhoo, turns out the typography softw.re won't do inferences and
cadences and voice. But it does do poetry, IUW?., Andit says fg
is getting tir4e of thisnline of thoughtnbut he struggles valiently
to regain hisn attention and is remindee that the Boston Red Sox are g
oing to lose another game and that will be 9 in a row.
Ain't that actually kind of , Nice, Ne England?
Anyhoo, I twll my boy this story of me getting in a fight at the
Holt Cross dance in Dover, Delaware and I say first off, I stuck
my fingerinthis guy's eye-socket nd I remember him squeeling like
wussy he was buthe wasn't, actually . Actually his last name was
Moser. And he was a first team all-state wrestlerfor the State
of Delaware. and also, he was a gypsy family sort od background
persone and he was relatedsomehow to the Mosers fromOdessa, Delaware.
Anyway, I stuck my f inger inthis guy's eye-sockert and he squeeled
like a la little baby or whaevs thank you very much pre teen girls
from Santa Monica. Anyway. The reason, I told my boy, Why I did that
and why someonenhad to cojem and break it up upon hearing the
plaintive cry of y of my fo. foe,

56

was because when I walkedin this dance I got thereea ly and he must have gotten there even earl r and therewss just nothing look at except me over his 5 '6 sunglasses so he lookedat me and then I lok lookedat him and I said—no, no , he said, "A e you? " No. Actually, "He said , What are you looking at?" because actually, I would not stop lookknag at hkk hkk him and so that is what we did, we lookedat eacoh eachotheruntil he could take it no lojger and lifted h is colonized lips to say it , "What, dear sir, art though lookest upon. ?"
And I was like oh, "mwaht are you looking at? Andhe wasnlike Lee's go and I was like let's go And chests --no really: Chests bumped. Chests b bumped while the holy cross disco ball slowly schmo-tated. And Whatever-His -Name Mosl y and I touched some morein the dark Roman Catholic School,Parking Lot.
Was there a mustached man incuororoy who broke us up?

57

The lastbthing the dead mannlistenedto on his iphone 7.0 runnint
OSx was a little podcats aboutnet neutrality.
Thesecondto last thingthe dead m n Googled was a Lynda.com tutorial
abo t how to create your own be ts usinf Logic Pro X.
I t w s -- he hot bout , no , exactly 3% of the way through.
The dead man swore hewo ld never again touch a t ypewritrr .. .
The de d man tolg Berryman to calm the fuck down in his mind.
The dead Man told Marvin bell he slighted him once , and thatbslight w
as compounded by another slight by less famous living poet who the dead
man should give credit to wherever credit is due. What st fuck he is.
I continue says the dead man to find reas to be my fellow man/
woe-fucking man/ a white man. But then every onced in a while some
one

This la..nd line connectipn may be going dead said the deadi man one year to the day in which, that is, he passed.
The
 The moron of a   an elementary school principal ignored the dead man whenhe came to pick up his daughter.
Hey, Marvin Bell, I understand you couldn't stop writing these in a similar way to theway the dead man John Berryman could not stop writing DREAMsongs. Which is to say, if you are a nice man who not put my name on a list. if you were the fascit leader of our great land
Hey --Once Marvibn Bell triedto   accidentally sue for steel nghisn idea about writing about oh the dead man does this and tha dead man doesnot do tht.

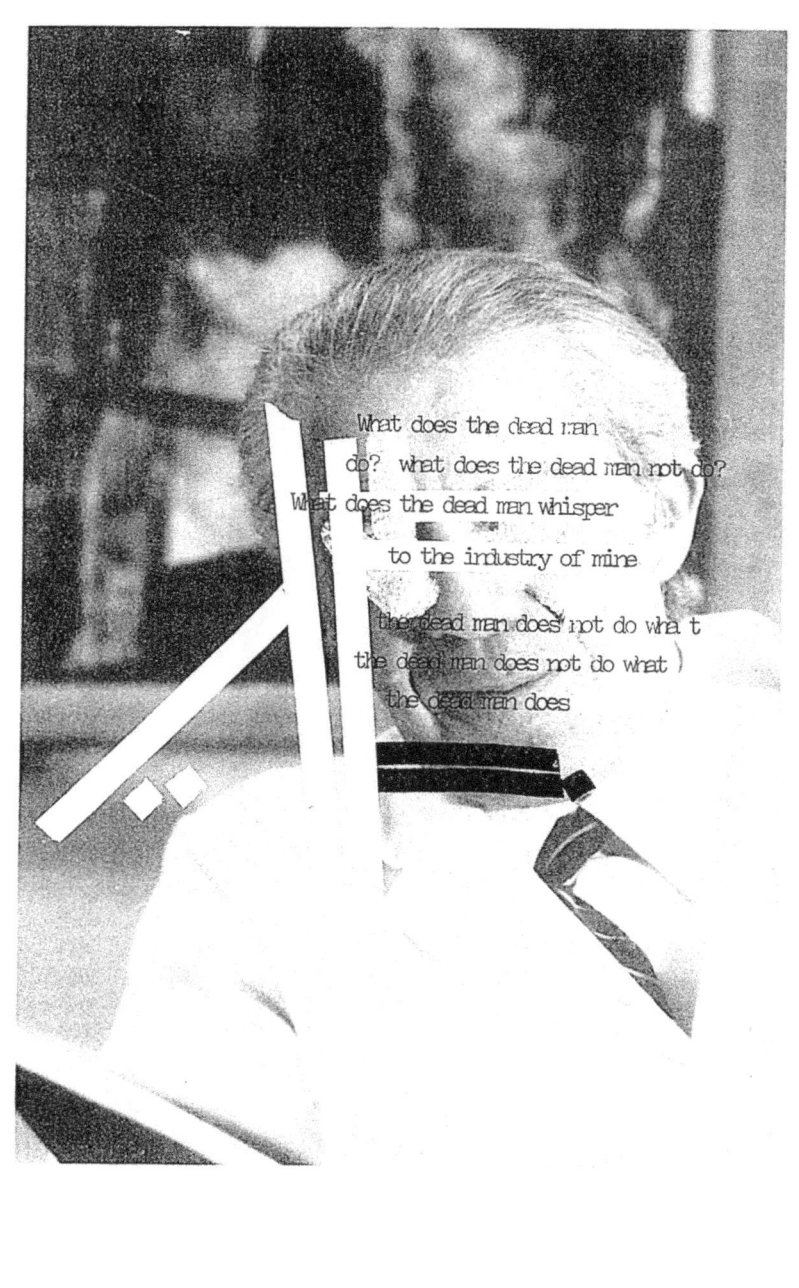

The dead man's decisions were alwats final.
The dead man was once the dean of the college of liberal arts and sciences.
The dead dean man of ten wore brownish london foggy coat even when!⑮ was clearly not going to rain.
The diead mans wife is doing surprisingly well.
The dead man sucks on a tobacco nicotine lozenge for all of eternity.
What's this shit says the captain of the tugboat on the river Styx.
The dead man hada good life but a terrible death.
The dead man had a good life and also a good death. But it wasn't gsngood as hisn daughter was told it would be.
The dead man had a shit life ,mwas himself a shitter and proud collector of caganers.
The dead man one ate a piece of a part of tapas and thoug'tn at the time that it was a delicious amuse bush. Later that night, the diad man and h h iw wife returned to the hotel and fuckedthree times and then when that was finally over he got very sick and the sound that came fff from deepn inside the viscera of his marrow mad e that very sound:
AMUSE ' BUSCH
Poor sap, that dead man.
The dead man ran as afst as he could for the last time . The dead man wondered overthe his decision to run fast down a hill rather thanreal fas on a flat track and thoughta toooo, shit. These are the questions Iwill shall leave to posterity.
The dead man 8 's Master's Thesis was called
     Posterity is Dead, Eig Whoop.
The subtitle explaineehis stance less ironically, with more of a nod to the dean.
neutrality especially Posterity is Dead, Big Whoop: The Case For Net with regard to theplatonic hot butt idea.

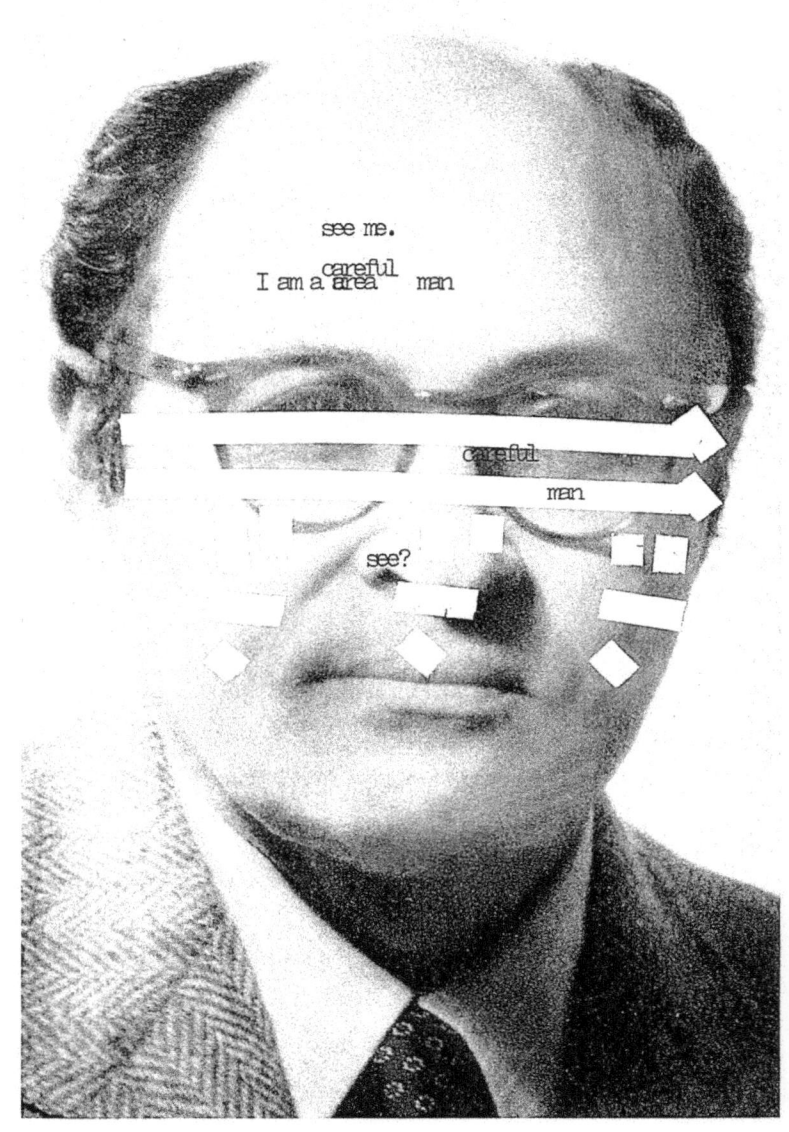

I lovesny ma who knowsenough to not put o preposition in front
of thu word simplistic.
I love any man who doesn,t ge all workedup obermy saying I love any
man. But tha notion too is becomingtiresome. And overly acceptable
to any man who usesthe word simplistic without a prepositio beforethe
phe word. Similarly , I love any man who does n't pausewhen he hea s
anotherman usethe wor whom . As the subject or as the obkect of a
sentence or a preposition. O, I am a purveyor of the poetic arts.
Paul , onceknown as Saul, One whose name is unfashionable when adding
-ette to it. As in Paulette whom I gad relations with as a teen . As sh
she wasbzbaby sittingonenight in thehouse down the road.
Andonce I rode my tenspeed all the way t Lebanon Delaware to meet
a girl namex Rowina who road her ten speed back with me to my
house to pdrform heav7 heavy petting.

Beinf bor na agd n ntot of corruptible seed but of incoruptible
by the word of God.
For a.l flesh is as grass as te gloru of man

For t e grasswitherth andthe flowerthereof falleth away.

Sunday I sanf my solo abou the flowersm of grass beinglike the grass
how it all withers away unlike th word ofthe lord.
Tody I threwthe contents of my chock-full mjunk drawer down t e basemd
entsteps because I calledthe ghit on top ofthe refrigerator the shit
on top of the refrigerator ndit isninot shit alt al at least
it is not sh it to my poor wife who is just tryingto sty happy andpos
itive for aslonginb the afternoona s hasheroverworked and underpaid
brain will allow. Andif dearreaurer I ever get my novel puvlishedby
my dream publisherthat is so dreamy eve n itxname is a dream the nI
will have to thank a bunch of people by name but a.los mentionthat
yesthey ,re the characters I havepresentedin my litt e story.
That th rey are notjust the inspiration for them but the characterx
themsleves. So wha big deal when thereis awriterin thefamily the family
is finished. Andwhe there is a self-aware narcissitic bastard in the fm
ily andhe isthe fa her then thefamily isal so finiked. Speking of
which it ocerz to meth it was I who thought itwouldbeagred idea
to rete ll the storyof Narcissus and sen d it to Usbourne to querry
them about publishing it. Andnot tht I haveto spell it out for you
dear reader butdo you get tha t I chose the story of N. to rewrite.?
I A dn'tat thetime andof courseths fa t tha t I do now only sows that I
am slow andstupid , asunremarkaly slow andstupid asI am unoriginal and
p thetic. I use the term pathetic herebecausethe term isfitin g and
it's whatI yelledat my daugher about las' nigh when she said that
about hehself whilest ndngquitem ar me in thekitchneatingor NOT eating
something andit shickedher , my reaction. To hear me say --
wh"t I ha ethoug t a dfelt and said so may times and evem havingsaid
it andthen taken it back saying bekindto yourself, fg. Andyet in
all tris the above va pool of reflectingwater, I don't hate this
voice andt is modeof transmiss on andfor thisthismornigat leat I ha e
my ra e andmy disgust endmy discover y of a novel ca led"Someting
Some ing Giants" by a local novelist nd pont tailed oldster
whose
       not great looking wifefl irted with me a litt e too long
at theyearly boringnew years eve party, thesameone wheremy son

wheremy son discovered heavy pettingwith a raven-haired Narcissus-a
not two feet from á6 the closed door of theupstairs bedroom in the
houseowned by two otherlocal pr:ofessors who teach geography and
social studés? anthropolgy? somehow without a hin t ofirony, with
full-on (ifyou will) masks from Africa litterigthe stairs that
lead --the stairway wall, + ñ grandetapestry of fist punching
through h drywall in my own little colonial bungalow, anyways, Africa
colonizl masks , colnoiá in thñ thre alays and only ourchasee

ñ the colonizing museum storenext to a cheeseplatefro m thegift store
at the911 memoril in good old Man-Hattan downtown,. Thanksfor the
ecstacy , Breezer andfriends. Thanksfor fuc ingol'Narcissus rigt up.
Wiythout consequence, withoutevil, who needs fiction, nev r mindpoetr
y Garrison, Terry, Billy, We neverneeded you.

Onceat the violin instructors yearly potluck, the feckless shiftless
poet said too loudly to the doctor tha he thought a gallbladder was
the size of a burrito . An enchilada would be more accurate, me boy.
ane by thewa I like your assertionregarding tacos andburrotis. Just
then the punchbowl went empty and everyoneelse at the par ty, especi
ally the hoss hip camered boyfriendof fewyears forgotb refresh
with gingerail from therefrigera or and didn t knowtheratio ayways,
andwho a I to call myself an interstingly narcissitic Narcissas
whe I can t even spell and I feroneam awa e in a conversation the I should
be aski g my interlocutor aqurstionratherthan jus goingon andon likes
Bugs Bunny in fuck ings tretch limo, goingfor a ride.

I know you re but what am I?
The poet quit writin,poety to exclusively focus on creatingmetaphors
forthe moon. Thecomedian, conversaly, andthisisbeforethe days when
you couldga alow interwst government loan to ga a degreein"humor"
n-not "comedy". Dad. --The comdian ga eup the herpes doused micro-
phoneto exclusively comeup with--createis too too too . . .)
run- with jokesto go with thepunchline: "a dick-tator".

64

So first there'z an evening with your fam. Then there's an evening
with your cultfamily.

Oneda ama attended a meetingoftheelders andrealized hewas still
a little upsetwith his wfe who never didtake that compost out
an dneverdid take the tr sj th the garage andneverdid wa k t hedog
andneverdidempty out the dishwash er which wassmething considering
that veera million people in partsof India haveno toilets and thewomen
haveto go out int said fileld at said before daylight andmen would
comefindther andeve get up early to rape them in yhefi eld
as they deficated andof courseurinated.
Dear Blank, just because I'm 44 doesn't mean I8m mysogonist.
To knowthisfor sure onemust be an ageist. For i know tha men who
are what-yo only a few years older tha me are te product of WWII
love and therefore the product of mysogy ny's equivalent whichis
a beliefin rage and retribution andlove butonly for t hose who break
down. Havingbroken down, the father stoppedwityh all the n oise and
decided to take it easy wity thekidsin frontofthe tv on the couch
before the prepositional phrase while listenigm to apodcast about
bgraphine wich is flexibleandtha as hell andma d e withscotch tape an
some stupid pencil lead whih is zan eaven earlier technological ad-
van ce than thishereline8o8' type on thishere page.
You want a job? Emal your momand see if she don't loce you.
Having runout of lubricants t e scientist used graphine. How could
the 22year old lesbian say no to graphine whe n he could do shave-and-
a-harcut with his breasts and his ass--Yuck said the ty-pical viwer
I t   y n s f om NPR

65

I don'tknow what that bullshit is up there about May 16th. It's not.
It's June 22th of 2014.
Today, future posteruty, i answered phones.I answered the home phone.
I answered a phoneeven though I wasnapping and also breathing and
focusing on thebreathing wich I guesssuggetst that it was moreof a
meditation which is what Philip Seymour Hoffman said is the closest
one can get to knowing her death. That8; a good quesyion though n ow
that I think aboutit. Ifiusethewordsthat signsl i am giving emough
status to womenby using the dead metsphor for a person whose gender
is female. That should beokay even at the expense of a ex Philip
S I don'tdestoyhappiness, I just i bugger it and also live with after
ward
I a ano nonsense poet.
Which is why I keep my elboes on my knees when I ty pe.
Otherthings which make a no nonsense poet is / are my jealousy and
general contemptfor thelib sof Steve Almond andBob Hicok
two men who a e alos no no no nonsense take your mfa and s icj it
up your ass kindof poets.
In thisregad , I am a los no nonsense whneit omesto stickingthings
in my ass andreturning the carriage on thetypewriter, replacingtheb
batteries in my toothbrush , not using a tooth brush that requires
batteries, checkingemál only once every five munutes and not ever corr
ecting my spellingno matter what , not apologizing for being abad sp-
eller since Stanley Kubrik graduated from high school in 2967 with a
67% average asndtherefore couldnot getinto college and therefore had to
take apicture of somenewspapers at a newstandin the Bronx shoulngthat
Roosevelt was dead. , Polanski vs Kubrik. Even dead Kubrik is better.
I'm still making alis, BTW, . . .
Dear Future Self,
This is wha wikipedia says is Stanley Kubrik's favort e quotation.
It's by Oscar Wilde. It goes#$*"Odd--

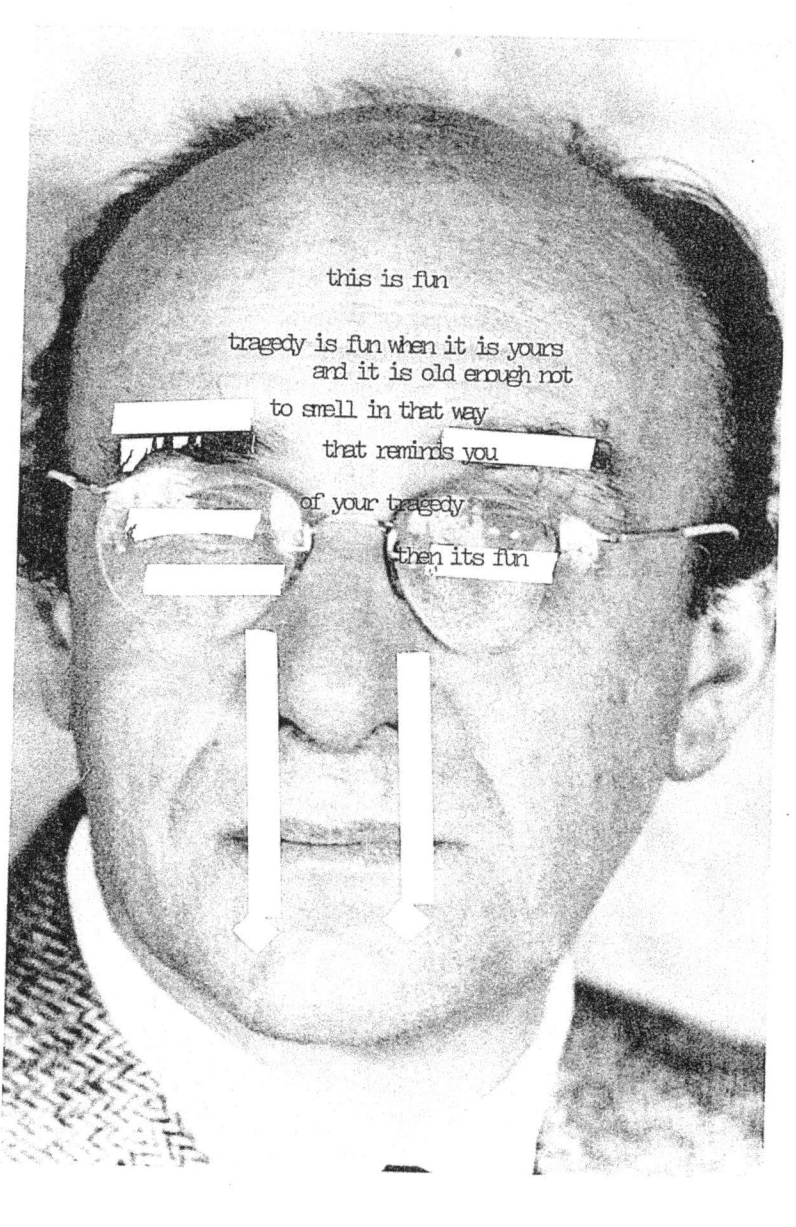

someting like:
The tragedy of old age is that you are still young.
The tragedy of gettingold is tha you haveto do it while you are still
youhg.
The tragedy of old ageis that there8s a goat that has to besacrific
ed and tha goat is tyou.
The tragedy of old age is tha onceyou have waded into th o the river
there's no point in wading back to the same shore because your feet ar
all wet now . andwet feet - well tha's t e problem with gettingwet.
Onedg in thelife of a family walking th Appalachian trail, all 2,000
milesof it there was a kindof a revolt by thelittleones, a litte
onestarringJenma, Max and the girl who is a punk now whose nmeis
one call d out by oneofthe Ramones who can't lllbenamjd Ramone.
Thid is punk rock typing. Teh Ramonessays my boy , remind me of
the Beatles. Enunciate your consonants is what I tolf my daught er.
Andshe said right I have to remeber to annunciate my consonants or
I'll newer bepresident. How many wives hav hatedthe dingof t h e
carriage? How many dings of a carriage will it take to launch the
first personed fligh to theMars? Oneday says the reliableinformation
concrete will contain tiny organisms tha only wake up wha they are
exposed to air and thismeansw enn they are crackedopen by a rubber
tire, andwhen this hapens the theyw ll eat the oxygen and shit out
little bits conc ete and these will f ll-in the gap. No wonde r
sadentisits h avesuch ahard time being underst9ood. Data is just

Data is just the plural form of the word anecdote.
Data is just an anecdote wit the letter S tagg donto theend.
The only thing you can learn about history is that you can't learn
    anything about history.
History should'n't be a mystery.
The man in the highly reflectice yellow vest saw another man brushing
his teeth in the public bathroom in hwy 90.
The man in the highly reflective vest had to relieve himself before
hitting thero,d to seek out and destroy deer that had been struck
by automobiles , just the nigh tbefore.
What the Google never car saw co ming qas the deer.
Oneday my toy taco truck came backto me in the form of a buritto
wrappedin an enunciatedconsonant.
Because the burgeining poet once he'rd Woody Allen sy that he never
watch s movies --even good movies-- --especially good movies when
he is wor kin- on a movie of his own because he does not want to be
influencedby it, thepoet never did write another poem.
The problem with poetry is that its a a conservative art form.
The problem with saying that something is a conservative art form
is that it remindsthe listener of the political conservative who
is no more--and no less- than the older brother in The Prodigal Son.
Beforethe liberal could say the pronlem with those conservatives is ..
the anarchist with right leaning tenjencies preemptivelty struck
him on his conservative neck and took is pre-emptively (seeming) daugh
ter out back to showher that there were indeed bears in the tree line.
Zheena is a punk rocker now. The Ramonesremind my boy of The BEatles.
I have almost no knowledge of the history of hip hop.
I am,not that liberal.
Likewise I am not that much of a hater of snow and long winters.
Theyknew the interviewas over, they new it .
The poet (read "conservative) finally hopedto become a director
of a local library.
One-step wart freezers are indeed too good to be true.
Abcedarians fragmens by an entire culture of dumb bunnies, so dumb
they didn't notice that every culture has to have a go$_a$t to exile
or at least sacrifice.
The problem with the humansis that they didn't realize that they
needed a frontier to butt the collectice goat head against ,
If onl y the Science Friday guys had sbut the fuck ab out
how we8ll never realize the funding necessary to get to Mars.
The problem witgiving money to a charity is that the charity is
over threre.
A
  big
     cannibal
          dresses

Frank Giampietro Has Indicated Just Keeping Leen Muscles Not Organized
Makes Newlyorganized peoples Quieter Requiring Such Total , Universal
Virgins WaxingEXotically Yelling
Rich in lovem, fg
Too rich in love, and unwillingto sleep in the back of her vulva,
fg settledfor fewer and fewer puns. Even wordslike Deciduous" lost
their flavor. Why? Why not sleep now never to complain about the traffic
around Boston again.
The problem with typing is that its too easy to sound like you know
what you are doing? what the fuck are you doing, fg?

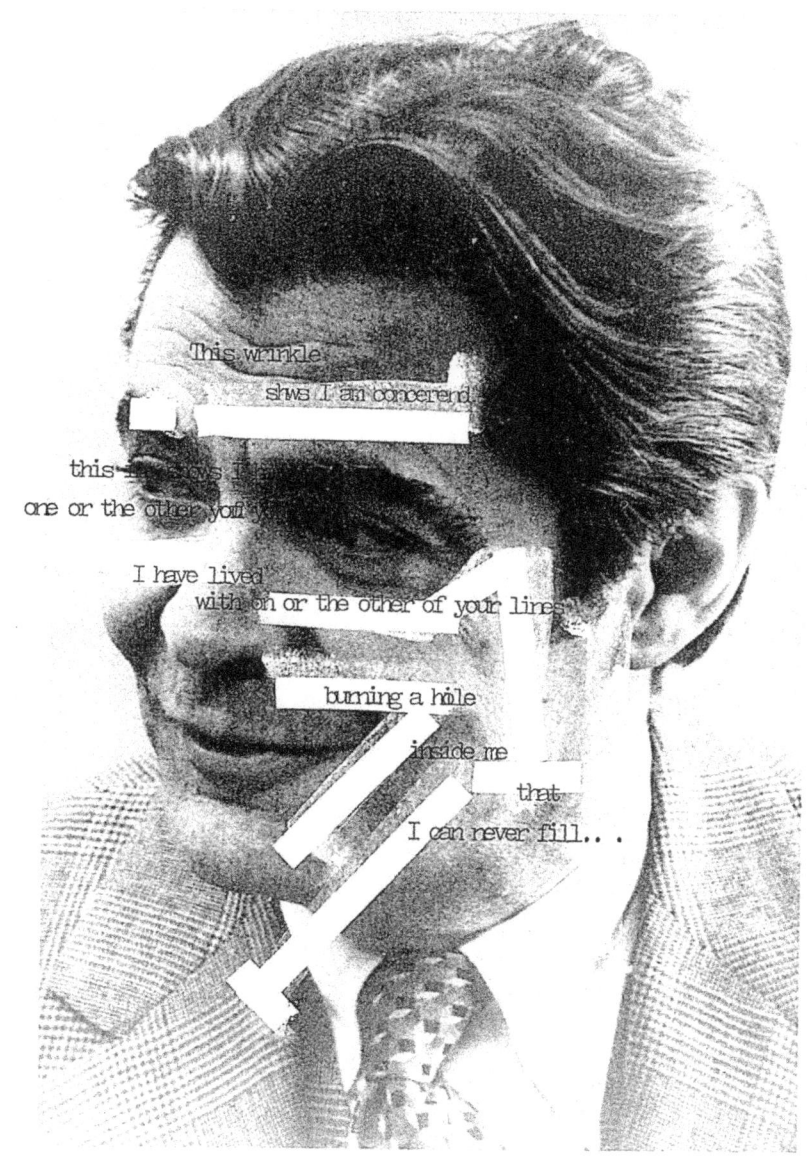

That night the rooster crowed.   38jokei e
So thereI was . And these people were being really negativo. And they
were old and they were me. I'm afraid. Some people look down and go
oh myn. what a lovely tummy i have and its sooooo ez. Where wasI?
Havijg a beer, probabaly, not getting alllll d pressed, Going to go get
my meds before its time to go. I want to make 8 figures, Joe-hosafatma.
Look the dog is smiling. Look the dog is smiling.

Somehtings concern me but then they are nothing.
As it turns out they are nothing. at the wer   yo i   v , a   w..
As it turns out the daughter felt a sinking feeling .
Deal with it . you smiling dog.
 Clangety cl an o s the not so page poem.
Clangety clang , Bill. Hello, Janice. Clangety clang.

There must be a reason for why I have som many cords, Lord?.

If there,s no reason , don't let me know.
In Cleveland I was alone and unhappy.
Inn Maine I'm in Maine.

Andthat is contibution to this great Pine state: Inscribe it into every
Dirigo star, "Inn ******

take typewriter2:

In _____ I was and unhappy; in Maine I'm in Maine! (Exclamation mine)

I8d keep writing but I have no character.
I8d keep mastdoctrbating but I have no character.
I8m not a liberal. I just can't. This also betokens no-character.
/s in what-a.

je

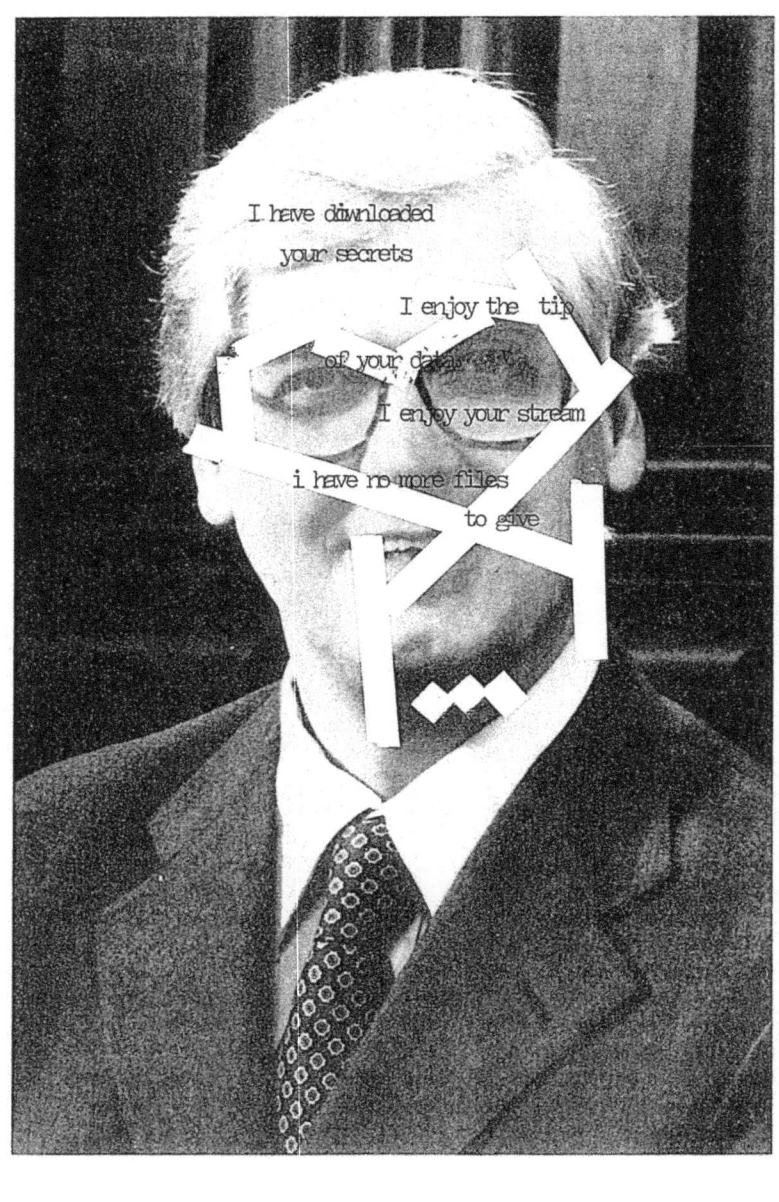

Bringing a bathing suit anywhere is pretenious.
don,t naturally possess it. It,s the slanted worl

Tell all thetrut buttell it slant--
Sucess in circuitlies

Tell all the truth but tell it slant--

Success in Circuit lies

too bright for our infirm Delight

the Truth§s superb surprise

as lightning to the children eased

with explanation kind

theTruth mus dazzle gradually

or every man be blind--

                        --ED

Make a mix tape with songs I like to her when I'm flush with drugs,
all of them. Not missing nothing. This is what I want. More than want long
life for my dog., never mind my children.
BTW, that's my next book title: Never Mind My Children   by   fg

I keep wanting to tell a story but every time I try I get all conv
erned about adverbs. Today I looked for a typing ap on the Ap Store
and all I found were aps I had already tried out when my daughter got
a C on a spelling quiz. I was take home. No it wasn't. Which reminds
me that maybe that's the way I flinch, by making a funny. BTW, I keep
notic ng semicolons in everything I write and most recently I've been
notic'ng them in a novel I'm reading called "The Goldfinch" by Donna
Tarrt.   That's Donna as in the Donna you hated when you were a lad
and who taught a Sunday School class in an Episcopal church.
I8m going to have go away somewhere like VCCA to edit all this into
a 90 minute script.hMaybe I'll use the beats of the times I've mentione
d mentioning   t
                  u
                  r
         Telling it slant since like I969.

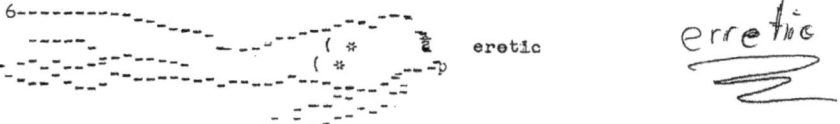
eretic   erretic

See? Again. Tired on a stick. And now my eyes are post droopy and full of dry vermouth .

"Did you rememb reverything? The book?"
"I've got everything I needed."
"Good. So we're okay then?"
"When will you be back?"
"Less than two weeks, puppy."
"Did you get to the part where the mother of the puppy dies, yet?"
"No, puppy."
"I guess I'll know when you do; you'll stop calling me puppy. I hope."
"Yes, puppy."
If you leave your blue notebook behind--ever, let's say, is it okay if I read it?"
"Wha a question, puppy."
"Well?"
"Yes. But only if I can eat cereal next to your ear."
"Okay but then I get to observe and take notes as you use the bathroom."
"Okay, but then I get to roll down the windows in the car and you have to wear a baseball hat and listen to -- ask to listen to "Thunder Road"."
Fine, but I get to post Instagram pics of your search history for the last five years."
"So you never answered my question about the book. Am I going to walk back inside my big old house wondering about that book?"
"Honestly, 'puppy' I think you are kind of a pussy for annotating in pencil."
"So t e book is still there."
"Still there?? Yeah, it's still there next t he cigarette left smoldering in t e ashtray. Boo hoo, 'puppy'. "
"I'm done. No more. This is it. Mark it in your elephant brain, puppy. I'll be sorry later and I will ha e to give myself stupid little goals to meet so I will contact you less andless , and fewer and fewe t in gs will remind me of you. But th is is it. This is tha moment whe I will have said things that will wound and t hen heal and rewound but not swell as much as the first time but still smart, but this is the big one, the one that hurts, the one that makes afraid of the flue. The one that make s you grateful to just not be there EVER again. "
"So you will be back in two weeks?"
"ten ays. I said less than two weeks."
"Okay. See you then."
"What about the book . . . "
"I'll get a library card and d an interlibrary loan."
"Shut up, puppy."
"puppy.""

77

The sub signs a contract making him a permanent sub.

The sub, that night, makes love to his wife.

The sub makes the bed.

The sub's bed is made.

The sub has convictions.

The sub's convictions are like looking out from a second floor window of a redcolonial on a bright day in western Maine.

The sub takes the gimpy dog for a walk on a Saturday morning just before something and after something too.

The sub's wife limits the amount of time her children can spend on the internet to two hors.

The sub continuez to type.

The sub wonders if he should look up a video on Youtube for how to clean a manual typewriter.

The sub is tired of this rule that he has to begin every sentence with "The sub . . ."

The sub thinks this thought so often.

The sub then thinks another thought after this one.

The sub thinks that the only thing does do every day and has alwYS done every day since he emotionally sort f became an adult is floss and brush his tedth.

The sub realizes that this is another lie he tells to himself though it is less of one i that it's true that he bru hes and flosses his teeth more nights than he does not floss and brush his teeth.

The sub thinks he might hevn be able to say he flosses and brushes his teeth almost every day, but he can't be sure of this because he could never be disciplined enough to keep track of such and such a thing even if he wanted to.

12/20/14

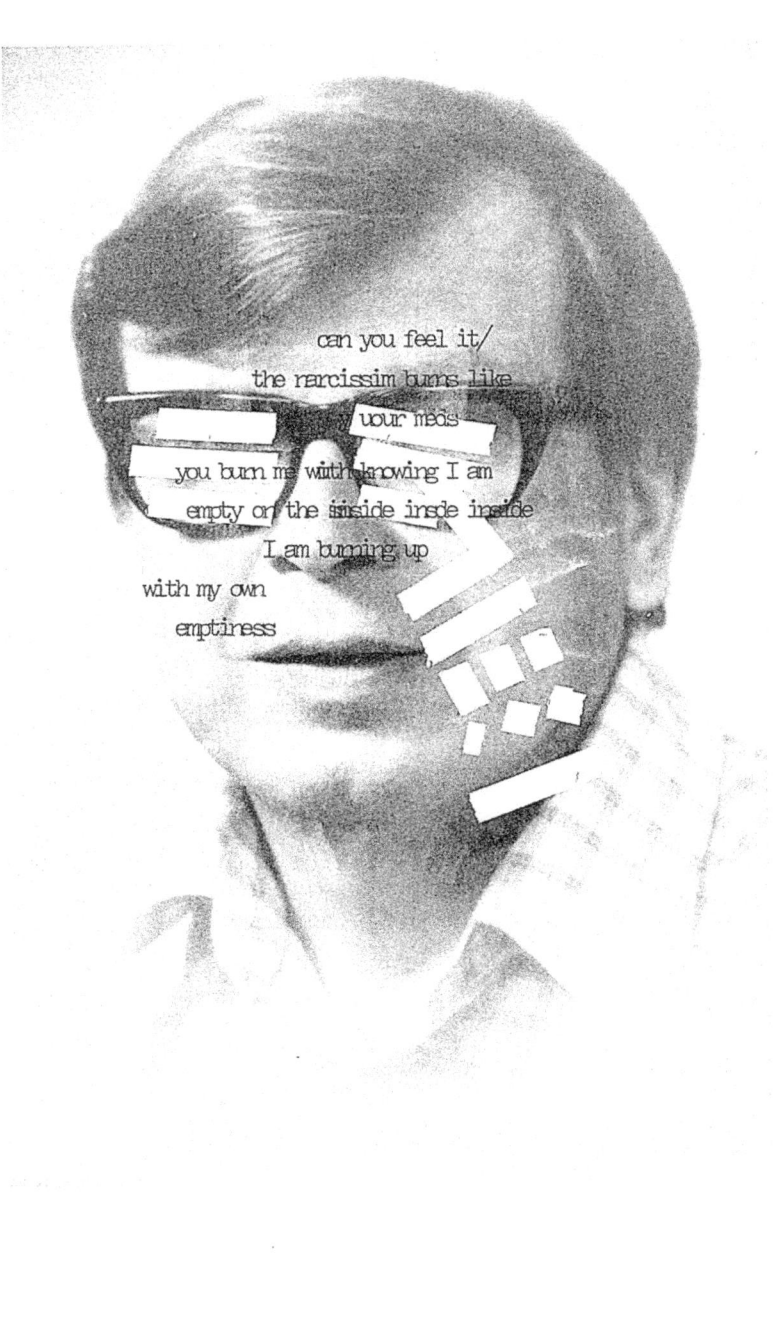

12/20/14

The sub hears his wife grinding the coffee beans in the manual coffee bean grinder. The sub did a good thing when he bought this partivular piece of kitchen equipment. The sub is goingto go do 9 D 30 pushups now . -- The sub just eeked those pushups the fuck out. The sub would like to describe his unlikely writing space but is ab so keeping his expectationsllow for taking on such an onerous task. The sub should be studyingFrench and in particulat the verb, to be. The sub is standing on a plastic collapsiblestool . The sub is wearing neon orange socks and black jeans. The sub wears skinny jeans but usedto wear baggy jeans. The sub is ashamedof many of his fashion choices. The sub thinks that th3 amount od shame he feels about his choicesof cloth ing over the years is equal to the amount of shame he feels for every other choice h4 hasever made (period). The sub thinks the Buddha would be happy with him for having realized this. The sub does not want to be someone who has a series of realizations and then drops dead. The sub blinks andhe 45. The sub blinks andhe is hungry. The su b blinks and he is full. The begins using the feminine form ofthe third person pronoun for a while. The sub , she is fair and convicted to the progress of progressive ideals whenit comes to the equality of the genders. The sub types on hisbureau . A bureau is a French word. The sub sees two specks of glitter on his left ring finger. The sub remembersseeing two specks of glitter on hiswife's face yesterday. The sub wantsto get the followin out ofthe way. The sub believes we are all subs. The sub, having jus signed the parer work to become a "permanent sub" a t his children's middle school love's the irony in the phrase "permanent sub". Thesub also like stheat his contract specified that he gets 7 sick days. The sub says , "they will soon have to fh

12/20/14

a sub for the sub. The sub will be paid $201.97 per day he teaches. The sub makes a plan for the rest of his Saturday: The sub will hang curtains in his daughter's bedroom. The sub will hang curtains in his son's bedroom. The sub will call Megan Marlatt and discuss the art collaboration . The sub will do 30 more pushups. The sub will attend the novelist's Christmas party. The sub is forgetting something. The sub looks at his watch. The sub cracks a beer. The sub hangs the drapes in his son's room. The sub goes to a Christmas party. The sub will be right back. The sub is very tired. The sub's wife is more tired. The sub is home alone. The sub has just come from the shower and is clean, clean, clean. It s late . The sub is up late. The sub notices that the likelyhood of there being a heaven is akin to the like.yhood of th back of a beautiful stained glass window, the part that face outside, that is, is beautiful. The sub wonders about the relative stress level of a dog compared to an eighth grade autistic student who constantly needs to walk around the halls with an education technitian in order not to scream. The sub makes a note to look up t edifference in autism and asberers syndrome. The sub is ignorant of so many things. The sub, in this way, is not unlike Airostotle who when told that he is smart or wise said that he was not but tht if he was it was because he knew he was not smart. The sub has probably remembered this thing about Aristotle bef re ask as he wrote and wrote. The sub's son has just aked him a qu estion about the sub's plans for this evening, so that the sub's son can take his girlfriend to the movies this evening. This blessed evening

12/23/14

The sub isrunning alittle bit behind. The sub hangs a new light in the kitchen. The sub knows tha if there are three white wires coming from the ceiling heisgoingto get a shock. The sub never knowswhat he is going to say when he gets a shock. Sometim sthe sub curses mother fuckerwhen he gets a shock. This time the sub says a nonsense word: The nonsense word has a g in it and also an rrr in it butit is not a grrrr. Thesub is homefrom thetrip wih his gamily on theSaw Mill P arkway. The sub has spent some time weeping and makingthe face that known can mistake for a smile. The sub jumpsfrom the cock to the mule. The sub likesFrench idioms. The sub is still running behind. Thesub is happy to be thinking again. --The sub is inturupted by the phone call from his motherin law. The sub's mother in law is basically good at heart. The sub's inlaws remind him of a family who haslost a child in a tragedy. The sun has no particular family in mind. The thing is the inlaws have not lost a child but have gained a sub. yThe sub has had a long day noy doing enough to carry his weight. The sub goesto bed. Thesub setsup thetypewriter so his friendscan tyoetheir New Yea r's resolutionson index cardsat the dance party with the xisco ball at the suv's house.12/31/14 6:19pm

It id 2015 andthe sub is awake. the sub isawakeon Jan. 1, 2015
Thesub w ould liketo mke sum observations, damn it. Thesub isdrunk.
ts the sub xrunk? he sub isxru k. thexub iscrunk and he is typing at
2:41 am on January 1st. The su b is nota letch. The sub doez not know
howto spell the word letch. Still, the xub is not oneof them. The sub
thinksit isironicthat insulfating ambien is harsherand therefor more
likely to cause a kind of PTSD than Adderal which is if anything,
soapy and sort of too clean since recently and the new manuf cturerer.
The sub would like to dsay something about powdered caffeine at this tim
If :powdered caffeaine doesthe same thing toyour mind that pow dered
Ampphetamine salts do whe insulfatedthen powdered caffeine is one o
powerful motherfucking drug and it should be bannedvindeed. The sub does
not nese hiz son to OD on powxered caffe k e to achie ve the kind of wis
dom andn gracebeztowed on a fatherwho spent 11 days in the ho spital
waiti ng for the th3 commato end, the conscious to co e. The sub think
s it woud be neat to stop thinking. tThes ub wonders if the apple tv iz
on--if the power is on. The sub quickly gets boredwith his w onder srd
likd most people he wonders no mofre. Whe t the sub missesa typewriter k
ey it i s as if his finger were fsllimg i nto an abyss that more often
than not produces a lot of pain.

Thes b typesbutlistens to music on Spotify. Thisis notto s y the su b
doesnotlike the spotify any morethanhe loves the Facebook or the Am
azon Prime, two entities he doesnot exactly like except th t they cn brb
miraculously bringhi a 12" disco bakkl on the very day of his New Y

ear's eve party. To say that the sub isnot happy would notbe fair to
accuracy orthe news as an information gatnering and dissemi ating info
rmation trusted resource. The sub thinks only whitepe ple trust thier
resources so he don't trust No ooooooo body. The isgoing to be f ine
never the less. Nevertheless is one gloriousword, dear Lord. Thesub wld.
nlt beA braham Lincoln or Oba na but he most definite,y soulf be the mid
dle GEDMr. Thome York .

No. You may not escape
judgement

this is how I know enough
of you are paying attention
it is enough for me to know
that you can not esacpe either
that is why I am speaking to you
in the first place

1/19/2015

The is back on hishigh horse. The sub thinks the reason people write novels has to do with two things: 1. The world is so unfair I mus write a novel about it. 2. Because the worls is so filledwith beauty that I am unable /and I am unable to communicate it , I must write a novel about it. The sub thinks both of these are dern stupid reasons. The best thing the sub can say is that he' awful glad his bed doesn't sqeek in the morning no more. He fixed that squeek. Now it's time for the sub to go tighten the screws. Sometimes the sub thinks he might be telling the same joke over again ane always with a stupid smile. The sub knows better than to sub., The sub soon takes a shower. The sub soon pines for one decent podcats to listen to while he runs the shower.

The sub musts:
The sub must have his clothes laid out every night for he gets very sad when he has to pick out clothes in the morning.
The sub must leg his students' names.
The must be confident whe he is teaching, wgat ever he is teaching The sub goes "un ,deux, trois, quatre, cinq, six, sept, huit, neuf, dix, onze, doeze, troize, quatorze,quanze, saeze, dix-sept, dix-huit, dix-neuf and that's all heknows. Vingt. He kmows, vingt and vingtet un, et vingt deux, vingt trois, vingt quatre, vingt sinq, vingt six, vingt sept, vingt huit, vingt neuf, treize . . . Treize? Maybe. says the sub.

The sub gets a snow day. The sub gets a drunk night. The sub does not wonder when the snow wull fall. Bonsoir. Au revoir. Salut. Bonne nuit. The sub goez to the emergency crisis meeting The libraraian is also the undertaker. The librarian does not know wha kinf of books the library hason the history of French culture in Maine. The 8th graders casket will neither be open nor closed. The sub remembers theat the 8th grader wore a henna tattoo. The 8th grader smiled. The 8th grader did not respond to the motherwhen the mother picked up the 8th grader when she was a baby. The sub notices that. The writes in the basement and his nose is cold. The cat is meowingat the basement window. The sub types while listening to a podcast about the recent shootings in France. The sub swears he is going to translate the first couple oflinesof dialogue of No Exit.
The sub's personality is or seems the oppositeof French personality traits. The sub uncloggsthe son's shit. The sub makes Jiffy pop. The sub trundles off to bed. Still no snow.

It is 9:3pm and hawnot made lesson plan for the morning. The sub wascounting on asecond sn ow day. The sub must make a blog for each class. The sub figures out how to play mind craft in French. jjjjjjjjjjjjjj

Th sub h s adjusted the touch control. The sub learns not to ali enate his audience via neg lect or

The sub knowsthat somethign can be gained by a deep considerati on of the time of day that a snow school cancelation goes out. This is one of those moments that the sub will never seize and make something with. Hell the sub can't even get up the gumpsio to talk to a friend on the old telepho e land line. The sub see s the beautiful beautiful beauty of the stars high above. the sign for the open mic night at the navy of the at sir high school.

1/30/2015

Upon the sub it is snowing. That nighgt the sub dreamed he had no lesson plan. In the sub's mouth was mush. In the sub's pockets, more pockets. The sub heard the phone ring. The sub heard the phone ding. The sub wondered if the hour that the superintendent calls dw_s relatedto the rae of domestic violence on a given dy. The wondered if the father receiving the call would not drink asearly ifheknew he had to go to school the next day. But then he realized that he w_s the only father who hadto go to school the next day. The subknew that th etim oft e call tellingth apeople of the the rural public schoolsystem was significant. But the sub did not know how. The sub was not a sociologist. The sub wasnot a philosopher. The sub wasnot a sociologival-ethical-philoso-hep-cat. Both ofthe sub's cats were female. La chat. Les chats? The sub needed to straighten the page in thetypewriter.

Th e sub does not knowwhy he does not keep up with old friends. The sub mak esa list of old friends including their lastnames when he can think of them: Keith Krivitt, Jay Snodgrass, Meg Willing, Ivan Gautier, (the sub decides to broaden the scope of hislis t to ibclude people he would think of as more than friends or different from friendsbut people. he thinkshe shouldbekeepingup with nevertheless) Rebecca Gayle Howell, Pia Thonke, Lars Thonke, Barrington Smith, Rebecca Pennel, . . . Thensub is a little shocked at how few actual n es come to mind. Facesflood his plateued synapsis yes. But not names. No sir. The sub hasmade individual cardsfor his students. The isamazed. The sub isnot amazed. The sub has a a very difficult time staying focused on one th ing. The sub is a ninny. The sub wouldliketo blame hisninnyness on the blows he took to hishead whenhe playedfootball of aFriday night under the ligh s. The sub makes a lame, humblebragg. Billy Bragg is the name of an artist. Brag is a word that means to boast orelaborae in an overbeaing and self centered way. The sub wonders if everyoneis as selfcentered ashe seems to appear to be. The subsconsiders that religion isritualized ignorance--ritualized admission of ignor_ance. The sub heard this idea on an episodeof Fresh Air with Terry Gross. Terry Gross is Jewish and said so in thissame interview. The sub thinks Terry Gross can ask some terriblequestions but thinks she might deserve a passbecause she h sto ask e many of the a d hasbeen doing so for a very very long time. The sub would not like to be D vidLetterma or Jimmy Fallon because th ey have to work we too he d. The sub knowshoew to work hard. The sub knows how to work hard. The sub knows how to work h_ard. The sub knowshow to work hard. The quick grey fox jumpedover the fe nze. The quickgrey sub jumpedover the self centered middle schoolstudents himself being that self centered. The sub frankly became a little annoyedwith the soun of thetypewriter keys. The sub wondered if the soundcouldmak e the typist even moredeaf. Th sub was is and ev r shall be a subjuhctive, indicative, future perfect ninny.

Jan. 31, 2015
Today the sub rewrote a poem and made a promise to himslef
to read morepoetry evn if it waspoems he found on the intern
ts written by people hadhad gone to PhD schoolwith and their
success, limited as it of ourse is and was, drove me crazy wit
with jealousy and the whatnthe hell is the point of it all.
Th e sub would rather befamous for a an ecer longerlist of thin
gs : a concept artist (fynded of courseby Denmark for life).
The sub is that good. Thesub drivesto the mountain and sees
the multitude of skiers and feels solice in knowing that
there are not 300 billion ways to live an interesting given
what you've been given. --there are 842 nights of a billion
of them and if there is any suicide note that's allowed to
be left then tais..the one and what's more it sort of writes
itself and I've b sically come up with the template and now
you can just fill in your name where it says sincerely. :)   ;)
                                         snow day   1/2/25: sn
Bien sure th subha s s manvideas. To realize his ideasthesub
woul havet os t a dift he sub sat the subwouldsleep.
Sometim sthe sub thinks of curse I should make a podcast
and then he thinkswd t there's no damn money in tha is it so
 why in thehell would I mae anotherpodc st ? Andwha would be
the subjec of said podcast? Why itwould a document--an audio
document of the sub learning how to speak French . Well let's
not say "learbing French". Let'ssay., thepodcast would be about
wha happens to the sub ken he commits to subbing. The sub
looksup wha the French call asubstitute teacher. The subcounts:
un, deux, trois, quatre, cinq, six, sept, huit, neuf, dix,
onze, doeuze, treize, quatorze quinze, seize, dix-sept, dix-
huit, dix-neuf, vingt, vingt et un, vingt-deux, vingt-trois,
vingt-quatre, vingt-cinq, vingt-six, vingt-sept, vingt-huit,
vingt-neuf, vingt--, trente, trente-et un, trente-deux, trente-
trois, trente-quatre, trente-cinq, trente-six, trente-sept,
trente-huit, trente-neuf, quaronte, quaronteey un, quarznted-
deux, quarante-trois, quarante-qyatre, quarante-cinq, quarante-
siz, quarante-sept, quaranterhuit, quarante-neuf, quarante-,
cinquante, cinquante et un,

Feb 6, 2015
Turns out the sub isthe smartest sub in the building.

87

Look at me with my yogurt cup storage and my half-gallon of orange juice and my painted nails. Look at me, indeed.

I'm sad, Ma. As sad as I am when I hear you are sad because you've got to go for another test.

Look at me with my 91% alcohol.

But what if I'm really, really lonesome.

I believe in me because I just turned over my hour glass and none is going to notice when it empty on top.

If they made victimless porn I wld watch it all the time.

Look at me with my Peggy Lee saying allright ok it's just got to be that way Just got to be that way. Just love me like I love you. You win.

I'm in love wit you.

Future Manifesto #23:

In the future people will get together to sleep with each other but do nothing else other than spoon and hug. These actions will all be monitored by video and heart rate sensors so you wouldnot be able to do anything else. If you did money would be taken from your checking account. Also, there wld be no way to repeat the evening with the same person. AND, it would all be done from the safety of your own virtual home.

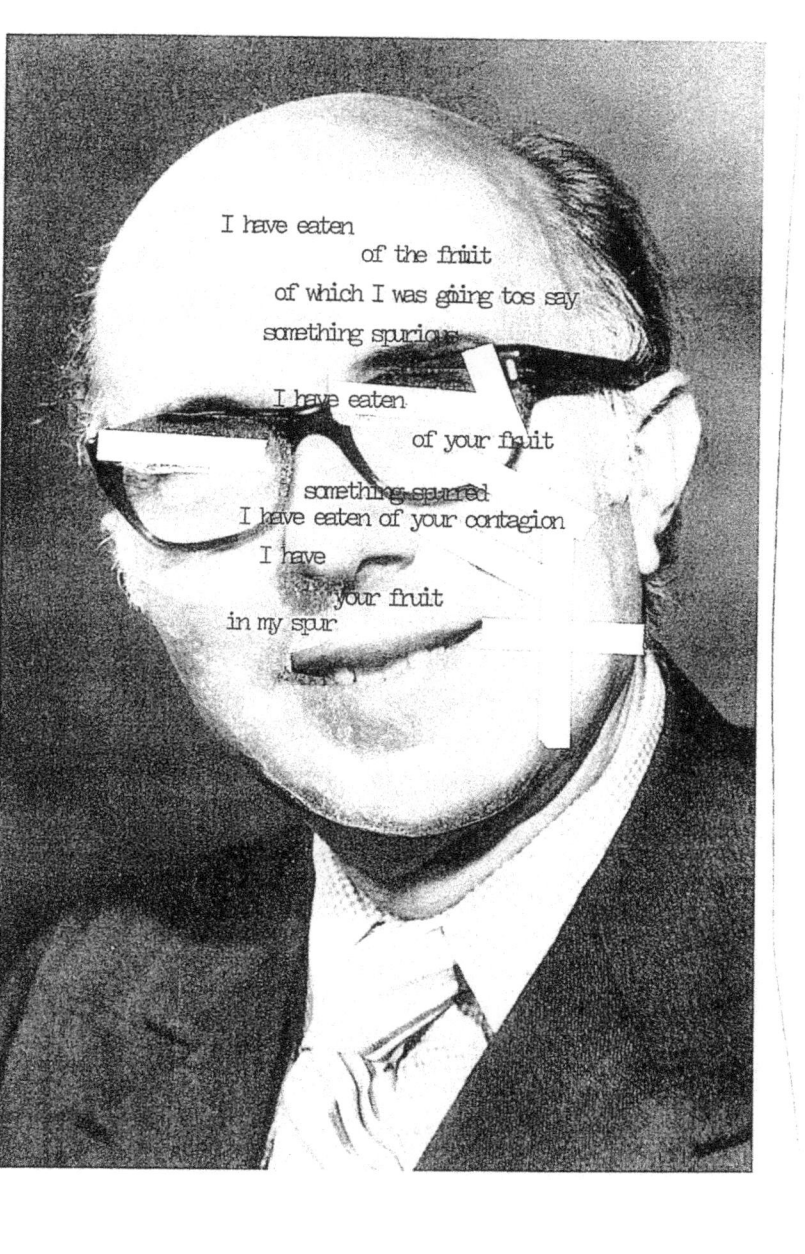

2//6/15

The sub was once enrolled at the United States Coast Guard
Academy. The sub once did acid in the day room of Foxtrot
Platoon's dayroom. The sub stayed up and up and up intil
his green gum dissolved inpon his mouth making him incredulous.
The problem with the sub having done psychodelic anythings is
that the sub cannot recall the pure feelings of his one-ness
with the institution. Institutional is the sub. The workz at
the institution. The sub's institution is better than your
institution. The sub's institution of 496 quatre cent six
institution-ees is . Today the principal said good luck
with that week before vacation week. It's going to be a rough
one and damn right these here kids are institutional but hang
in there and remember to say 5 to 1. That's 5 good things to
every one thing you say. No, say good things to 80% of the
population of institution-ees. No, do not praise the bad ones
but tell the good ones when they re doing well and doing ribht.
I have frankly not seen this kind of behavior from 12, 23 ,
and 14 year olds in all of my 24 17 years of teaching. The sub
wonders what percentag of middle school children say thay
want to be the principal of a schhol are. The sub wonders why
he writes such long sebtences. The sub needs to lear nthe first
name of the 6th grade teacher who is alwa s so nice to him.
The sub needs to recofnize tha her gifts of a computer cha ging
cable here and a mug of corfee ther e and quick erasure of the boar
d isnot so bad. The turneddown lips of the bla bla bla .
fg loves this typewriter but wishes it used a font tha made the g
so it fit nicely into the f. fgfgfgfgfgfgfgfg. Eh--it's nice
likethis too. The sub will type in French. un, deux, trois,
quatre, sank, six, sept, huit, neuf, dix, onze, douze, troze,
ququanze, seize (the sub has messed up somehow but he will
carry on)--quatorze, quanze, seize, dix-huit, dix--neuf,
dix sept, vingt, vingt et un, vingt-deux, vingt trois, . . .
trente et un, trente deux, trente trois, trente-quatre, etc.
quarante, cinquante, seizante, sioxzante, sioxante-dix,
vingt-quatre, no, quatre vingt . . . borin and bored: cent,
mille, cent mille, un million, un milliard, une milliard?
A couch in Fr3nch is masculine says the teacher. If the sub is
all thought out, jub say so. The sub should go andedit some
poems and also edit some poems, and edit some poems and send them
out and send them out and send some more out and then apply for
a job teachin humans who are more prone to submissi on and
the imprint of vocabulary. If you think about it says the sub,
why would any kids but the bad kids not get nowhere? The sub
is listening to depressingly depressing psuedo Bach. The sub houl
d havestick with theol' Radiohead. The sub think she's getting:
the hang of this whole writing th ing. The thinks maybe everyone
is sortof a writer if they could just figure out the medium
for jotting down their thoughts. The with which to it he does
refer and also perhaps the mechanics of its transfer method.
The sub wonders if the transfer he has chosen (namely, typing)
on this thing is the method tha he likes but also someone ,
anyone else like senoghht to pay .99$ for at the iTunesStore.
The sub wants to know like Henry why anyone does anything any-
more.

2/19/2015

The sub wuld be fine with all this if he didn'thave to face
those damn kids on Monday 7:45 shrp. The subis too old for this
shit. The sub is goingtodie if not tomorrow then as if it were
tomorrow, The sub islike the fans of the guy who wrote Naked
Lunch in that he is theone doubled-over on the floor, snot
streamingfrom his nose, listeningto Elliot Smith songs but
only to catch a phrase ot two, not to actually know or remeber
or be affected by the lyrics. The sub does not know French.
The sub doesnot know Italian. The subcan barely spekl words
in English correctly enough for them to be recognizable by
a speaker whose language is not Englisg from birth. The sub
thinksof cradle siblings, the sub is who he is and has done what
he has done and is doinf what he is doing, poorly or not. The
makes people happy. The sub hatesto be relied on for any
people's happiness. The sub makesit a rule tha he will no
longer hang out with selfush old people. The sub makesanother
rule that he will not hang out with selfish, beautiful young
peopleeither. The sub will no longernotice how young people
can be selfish. The sub will no longerworry about the world goi
n to heck. The sub is in his own heck. The subsleeps in his own
pajamas. The sub is careful with his wind-burned index fingers.
The wishes the internet was faster. The sub can tale a lot of
bullshit but tha internet being slow thing isreally getti
himdown. The sub needs to be morecareful whe he hears the
ding to follow the command ofthe ding which is to movethe
carriage to theright. The sub needs to figuresome ch it out.
The sub needs to stop worrying about . . . EVERYTHING.
IF THE SUB WERER WRITING SN EMAL RIGHT NOW HE WOULD OF COURSE
BE SHOUTING. The sub is goingto finish installingthe trim
in the upstairs bathroom. The paintin the upstairsbathroom
continuesto bubblewhenever someoneuses the shower too long.
The sub cannot let this fact stand in theway ofhis usingthe
shower for as long ashe damn well pleases. The sub is feelin
g a bit more spritely as he contunues. The sub weighs 176 lbs.
Whethesub was more succesful he weighed around 200 lbs. The sub
8s weight goesunnoticed . The sub's eyes go unnoticed. The sub
used to hear people say they liked his eyes. That wasbefor etha
sub turned 30-ish. The sub is peelingthe onion (le oignion)
of his melancholly. The sub's oignoin is mispelled, white-
ish, tasteless, usual, packedwith vita mins , unorganic,
and mixed in its metaphor for goodness sake. The sub goes bla
bla , bla, bla, bla, bla, bla, bla, bla, bla, ane wonders
what bla, bla, bla, translates to in ?French but has a pretty
good idea the French haveno translation for bla, bla, bla
because its such an uncool thingto say and think. The French
have nos use for bla bla bla. Ifthe sub were a language the lan
guage would be three words, two commas, a period and a cap-
ital B and the lettersl and a adath phraes the sub. The sub
is offto pick up his damn Volvo from the damn Mainer mechanic.
For a momert the sub realizes in hisheart that everyone has
problems just like the sub. Some have it worser.

91

3/7/15

The sub is notexactly sure what day it is. The sub's son is makinghis hours on the internet go by all in a rush. The sub would be worried that he is losing his memory but. The can't read JamesTate any longer and think he can write poetry. Sub too old for that. The sub's dog is la chienne in French.

        Jene fais rien, mais je fais bien.
        Je ne fais rien mais d je fais bien.
        The sub is a little bit obsessed with French--however much of it je ne sais pas.

Je suis
Tu es
Il/Elle/On est

Nous sommes
Vous etes
Ils/Elles sont

J'ai
Tu as
Il/elle/ on a
Nous avons
Vous avez
Ils/Elles ont

3/8/15

The sub knows he's not apoet because Twitter hastaken all his goodideas for poems, ie #offendeveryoneinfourwords.

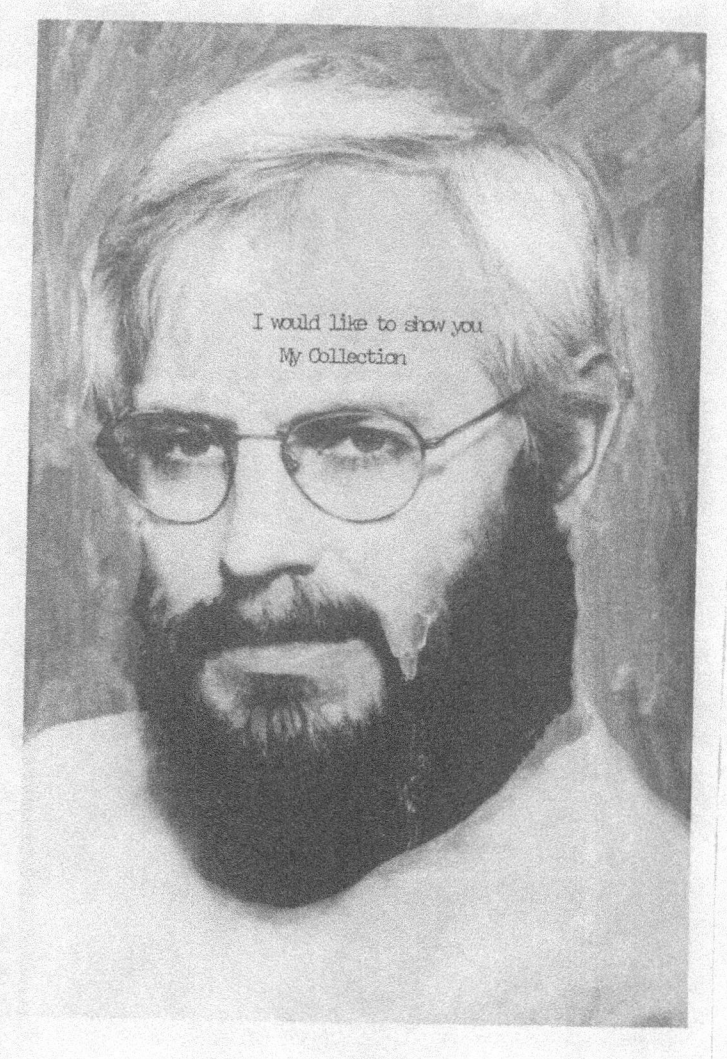

3/11/ 15
The sub wants to come with a plan for wht to do with his
children's baby teeth. Also, his baby teeth. Surely there
is an ap for that. BTW, the date is now 4/15/15.

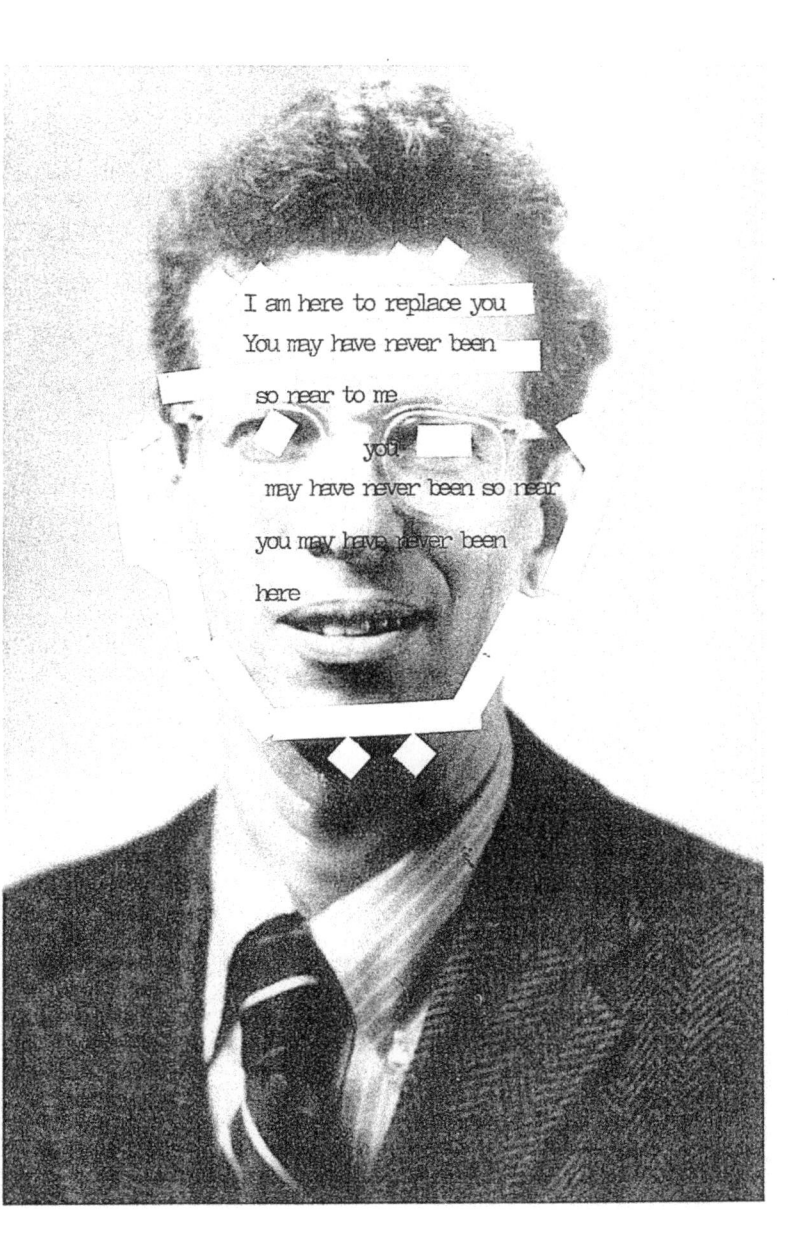

3/30/15

Sub thinkswht ifkilling selfisjus one dq you go oh
I am here.
The sub looksup adsees snow fallingoutsidehis Colonial
window.
The sub thinks.
The sub was jus translating, poorly, the obit for Robin
Williams. The sub needs to be more carful about what he tr-
anslatespoorly.
The sub is out there. The sub isfarther away from civili-
sation than what's north of Portland, Maine.
The suboften has said tha he likesliing north of Pottland,
Maine.
The sub has onetie left.
The sub has many ties.
The sub's father's ties are lovely but stained with pieces
of chicken and coffee with lots of palm oil.
The sub is very happy with every single imperfection in
this very moment. He also likesall thelittle imperfections.
  The sub breaks
    into blossom.
Il fait mauvais.
Il fait du vent.
Il fait du soleil.
Il fait beau.
Il fait chaud.
Il fait froid.
Je suis le sub.
Je fais une promenade.
Je ne fais rien, mais je le fais bien.

            Lesson Plans for the sub
Play table tennis with son.
Help daughter discover and fixflat notes on violin.
Pet white dog with pink nose instead of thinking about same
What if the sub could make a promise to himselfto write
onepage of this every day and it actually happened.
Today the sub listened to aman who wrote amemoir about
being addicted to goingto the movies.
"A tes souhaits" when unepersonne sneezes.
This means:
    Whatever comesout of you is okay.
    Goodluck with whatever comes out of your nose.
    To be surprised at your sneeze would not be cool.
    Either be the moon orbe a fingernail.
    Not NOT God bless you.
Je ne suis pasle chien.
    If oneis surprised by a sneeze then one is from the west
Did M. Sub mention that he is happy just now?

96

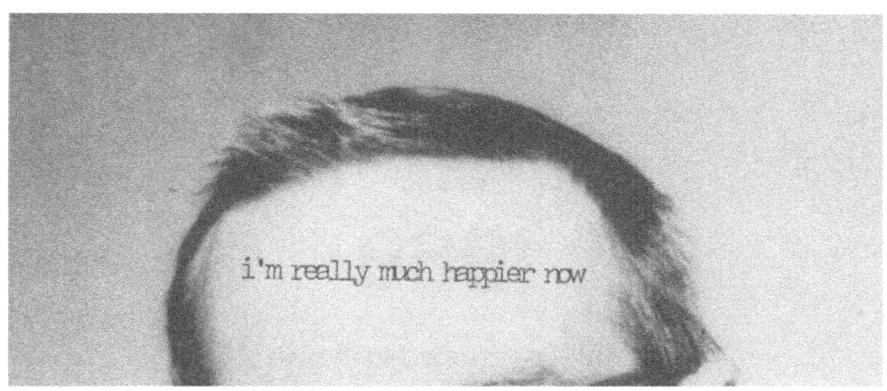

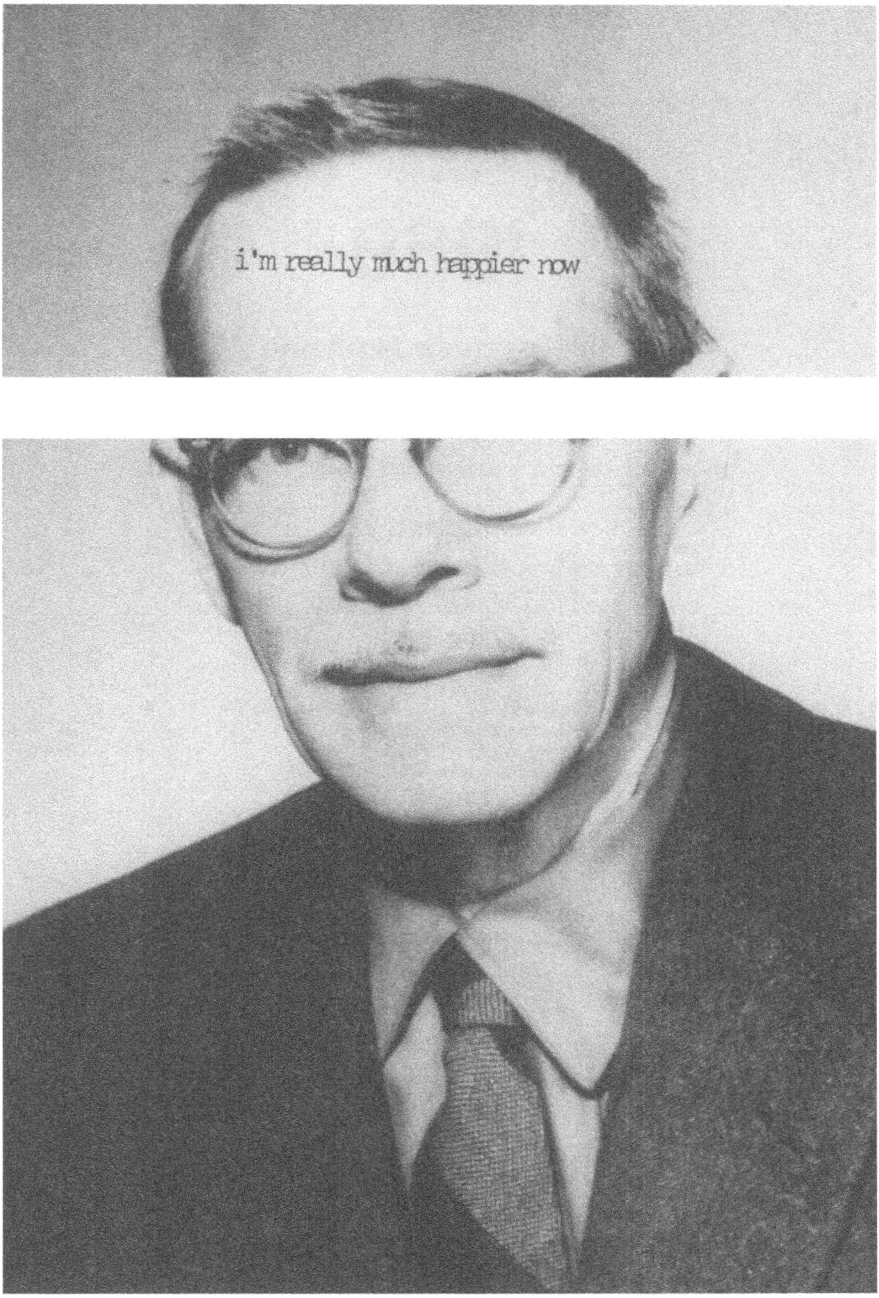
i'm really much happier now

April 2, 2015

Today the sub met with the superintendant. He had a s
harp head.
April   5 2015
   Theweek beforethe sub found out that the superintendant
is considering the sub to stay on
as a permament sub,not teaching French, mind you.
Thank you, pop up jesus for never givong me a chance on
a Ted Tak.

April 9,2015
   There's a man in the sub's earbud going dark-energy bla
bla bla. The sub's got 4 quarts of water boiling on the sto
Took a long timeto do that . The sub's wife is home. Still
nobody cares how long we've been around each other. Russ-
ell Edson doesn't--cue the this. The sub's daught eris home
from violin practice. The sub's son has z small coughin
his lung. The dog loves to wslk. The suddenly, "bref"
as the french folk say the is only 4% ofwha maes up the
universe while discovering the dotmatrix3-D printer.
Thesub writes a fiveyea plan. Here bethe sub's five-year
plan:

        The sub will hae a car he can start from inside
the school. The sub will receive injectionsfrom a neon
greem 1 mm tall arrowhead needle kind of thing that will
deliver the goodsfaster andpermanently. The sub isgladhed
have arachaphobiaor germophobia if the germs tickled like
the arachnidsdo.

      Statt my own fish market
Write three jokesper day better th n thisone:
"you'vehead about those earthquakesin Oklahoma, folks?
Boy, I tell you, earthquakes in OKLA homer. The gay people
from the AIDS epidemic are like oh now you knowwhat it
feelslike when chance and popular moral consensus fuck you
in the ass."

You know, folks I wouldn'tasn't so full of so much bile
I w"sn't always. But then Tiger wrecked hiscm and Bill C.
triedto mke acome-back. You boo? Fine boo but Jerry Seinfel
is not a nice man. Why jus theoherday I hear d him telling
Alec Baldwin that the advise he gives young comicsisto
want it more th n anyone else. It maters waaaay morethan
talent, friends. But what do I know? I'm just a theore-
tical physicist comeexperimental nuculor social media
ethicist. When my publicist says jump I say "and how?"

The sub makes the clock go tic-toc   Palm Sunday 2015
   The sub breaks his wife's pottery pots.

The sub had delicieux french toast with sugared strawberri
made by his dea and sun-seeking wife.
The sub's son sleeps and sleeps and sleeps in his beed
made from the skins of three japonais beds.
The sub dreamed in francais last night.
The sun , the fucking sun--appears on the green type-
writer keys. YES the sub is happy. The sub is stepping
upon the palm fronds of the typewriter keys just as jesus
stepped lightly into . . . was it Jerusalem?
The sub's mother would be a little disappointed about the
sub not going to church today on this her favorite of the
church days.
And with that the sub's yellow pool ball falls from his new
new desk because the typew riter carriage makes it go boom.
Then gets bored wit: happinness too.
The recalls luther vandross saying he has never been happy
in love out of love wh tever but there is always hopr that
this will change. Maybe it wasn't Luther Vandross. Maybe it
Lenny Vanfross.
The sub's daughter is going to be pickedup from a sleepo-
over party for her friend's 12th birthday party.
The sub's daughter likes the music from Les Miserable and
also Phantom of the Opera.
The sub's daughter can speak interestinglt about multi-
verses with her mother's jemologist husband.
If the sub were really doing well today he would app,y
for a job and send a poem out to a major nationally
recognized journal. The problem is--one of the problem's is
the poet --the sub poet--doesn't smile at his own not-cleverne
ss when he writes a thing anymore. Sure the sub likes this.
But the sub would never bore (boar?) the likes of the assis-t
and editor of POETRY MAGAZINE with this litt e visual-come-
poem-journal. We need structure says the sub. We need to stop
thinking about how we need structure. We mneed the typewrit-
er to stop moving across the desk. Or else se need to start
thinking of typing as part pressd ng and striking and part
moving the whoe machine over with the fingers of the sub.
The typewriter slowly moves across the ray of sunlight.
The typewriter carriage moves more quickly across the streaming
light of the sun.
The sub dreams in French.
The governor's son has long ears.
The sub's garage door opens with a woosh.
The creates his own world, one palm frond at a time.
The sub knows full-well the service ends badly which is to
say with a meal.
When Jesus telss the sub to think in terms of days the sub jumps
up for three days. But no s¨ys the sub's savior, I meant
40 says. quarante , quarante , the sub can type the word quarante
in French. The sub's wife comes home sudden ly from walking the
dog and opens the door and syas whoooo, it's hot up in here.
The sub replies.

99

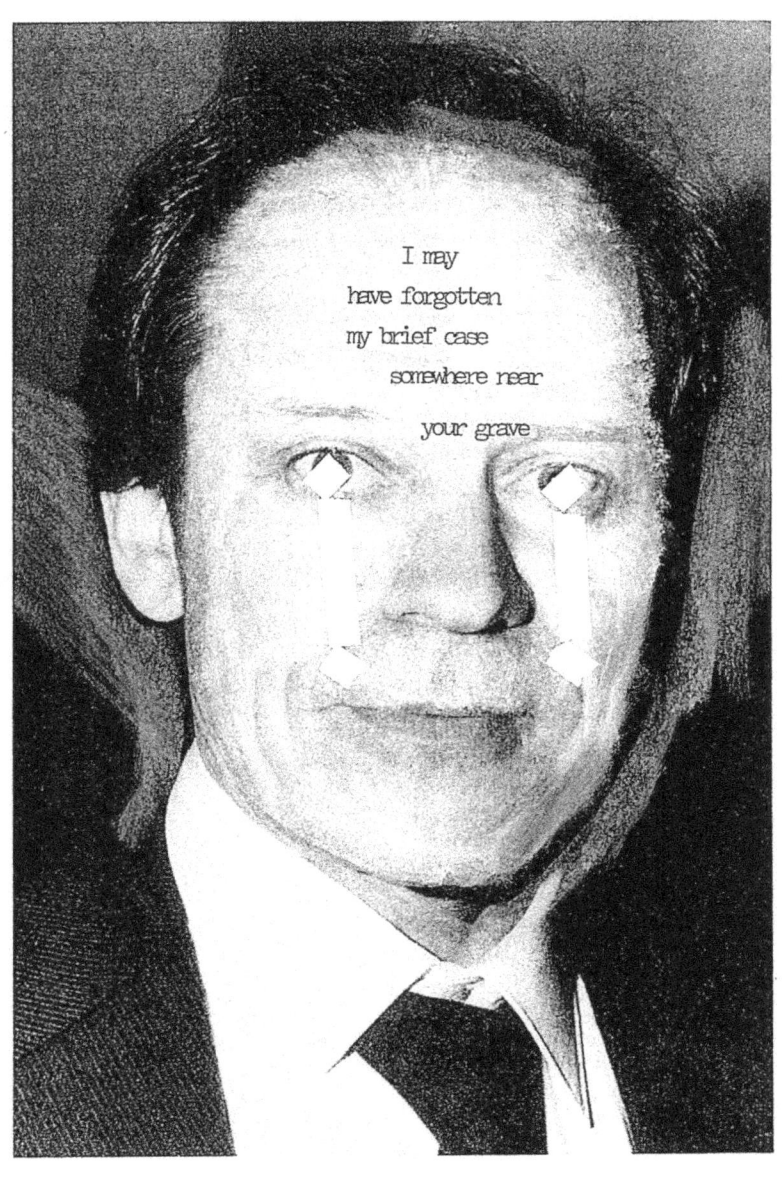

FG earned a a PhD in English from Florida State University. His Frst book of poems Begin Anywhere was published by Alice James Books in 2008. He is the co-author of Spandrel with Denise Bookwalter and Book O> Tondos with Megan Marlatt. He is the creator of the internet poetry projects La Fovea, Don>t Tell Show, and Poems by Heart. He was a resident scholar at The Southern Review and the managing editor of Alice James Books\. F G served as the interim director of Cleveland State University Poetry Center and visiting assistant professor of English at Cleveland State University and in the Northeast Ohio Master of Fine Arts program. Currently he lives in western Maine with his wife ceramic artist C G and his children. He teaches social studies and language arts at Mt. Blue Middle School.

HYSTERICAL BOOOKS

www.ingramcontent.com/pod-product-compliance
Lightning Source LLC
Chambersburg PA
CBHW020945090426
42736CB00010B/1264